THE EPIC
OF EDEN

JONAH

OneBook.

THE EPIC
OF EDEN

JONAH

SANDRA L. RICHTER

 Seedbed

Cover design by Strange Last Name
Page design by PerfecType, Nashville, Tennessee

Richter, Sandra L.
 The epic of Eden : Jonah / Sandra L. Richter. – Franklin, Tennessee : Seedbed Publishing, ©2019.

 pages ; cm. + 1 videodisc – (OneBook)

 An eight-week study of the book of Jonah.
 ISBN 9781628246865 (pbk.)
 ISBN 9781628246902 (DVD)
 ISBN 9781628246872 (mobipocket ebk.)
 ISBN 9781628246889 (epub ebk.)
 ISBN 9781628246896 (updf ebk.)

 1. Bible. Jonah – Textbooks. 2. Bible. Jonah – Study and teaching. 3. Bible. Jonah – Commentaries.
 I. Title. II. Series.

BS1605.55.R52 2019   224./920071   2019941783

 Seedbed

SEEDBED PUBLISHING
Franklin, Tennessee
seedbed.com

CONTENTS

Week Six: A Second Chance / 69

Week Seven: A Compassionate God and a (Very) Angry Prophet / 85

Week Eight: Does Jonah Get It? / 105

Group Session/Leader's Guide / 125

Video Notes Guide / 151

ACKNOWLEDGMENTS

As always, these Epic of Eden studies are dedicated to all the students with whom I've had the privilege of learning this material. Over the years of this curriculum's development, I have been so blessed to teach the greatest fish tale ever told to such an array of people, and have been so gifted by the insights of my students as we have grappled with who our God is and what he requires.

I want to acknowledge Kathy Noftsinger's unfailing aid in editing and helping to create the inductive portions of these studies. Her dedication to these projects is a major reason that they morph from vision to video. Holly Jones is the muscle behind our projects and all of us at Seedbed owe her our thanks for her production expertise and ability to bring all the parts together into a final form that changes lives. Our videographer Jonathan Edwards and Seedbed content editor Andrew Dragos made miracles happen in the studio. Nick Perreault, our cover and slide designer; Kristin Goble, our typesetter; Maren Kurek, Amanda Sauer, and Tammy Spurlock, our editors, have all contributed their talents to making *Jonah* come to life. Always a special thanks to Jody Brock for making sure my hair looks good and my heart is light. To J. D. Walt for his vision and his long-journey friendship. To our director of publishing, Andrew Miller, for his leadership. It takes a village to build a study—and every one of these people is responsible for the final product that is *The Epic of Eden: Jonah*. May God bring the increase! And to Steve, Noël, and Elise—my long-suffering family who has paid the price of too many late nights and weekends away to bring this curriculum to its current state—my forever thanks.

Introduction

What typically comes to mind when you think about the book of Jonah? A children's story? A fable? A legend? Or maybe it is the kids' camp song— "Who did, who did, who did, who did, who did swallow Jo-Jo-Jonah?" Most likely, what comes to your mind is a story that you've heard so many times, there could not be anything else you could possibly learn from it. Well, this study is written to prove that assumption oh so wrong! Here we have the account of a professional holy man. Someone who has spent his life and career in ministry, but who himself has not yet fully understood his own calling. Here is a lifer in the faith, who's about to have his very predictable God turn him on his head with an assignment he could never have imagined. In the words of VeggieTales creator Phil Vischer, this is a prophet who did not get the point!

If we move from the pew to the academy, we find that many interpret the book of Jonah as an allegory. For those who take this latter course, the standard read is that Jonah is representative of Israel, the whale is the nation of Babylonia who swallowed up Israel in the exile, and the trip to Nineveh is the conversion of the Gentile world that resulted from the dispersion of the Jews out of Babylon. (That would be the part about the whale vomiting Jonah up on the shore!) One of the great early church fathers, Augustine, had a more Christian take on the allegory: "As, therefore, Jonah passed from the ship to the belly of the whale, so Christ passed from the cross to the sepulcher, or into the abyss of death. And as Jonah suffered this for the sake of those who were endangered by the storm, so Christ suffered for the sake of those who are tossed on the waves of this world."*

Often folks read Jonah as a parable. Like the parable of the good Samaritan in the New Testament, the idea is that the prophet's audience is being taught to love their enemies, the narrowness of their nationalism is exposed, and God's universal goals for evangelism and conversion are revealed. Although these lessons are clearly present in Jonah's story, identifying the book as a parable also identifies it as intentional fiction—a problem for those who are also identifying Jonah as a historical figure. The phrase "popular legend" is also used in the study of the book. There are several reasons for this, not the least being that, hey, there's a guy *swallowed* by a *whale* in here!

But there is another much more biased reason for the reputation of fable, allegory, parable, and legend that often accompanies Jonah's book— and that is the perception that although the book *claims* to be from the eighth century BCE, its message to step outside the narrow boundaries of nationalism and reach out to one's enemies is too advanced for an eighth-century Israel, and therefore the book must actually be from the fourth or fifth centuries. Why the fourth or fifth centuries? Because this is the era following Israel's return from the exile. And many would say it was the exile that dismantled Israel's own sense of nationalism and put them into direct contact with their enemies. In other words, some conclude that the global vision of the book could not possibly have been penned in Israel prior to the exile.

But the God of the Bible is very much in the practice of challenging his people with counter-cultural messages that call them to be more than they think they can be . . . to stretch them further, push them harder, so that God's people can be more like him and less like this world we find ourselves in. So if you actually believe that God can do such things (challenge his people to reach beyond their cultural comfort zone), it is not necessary to

---

*Augustine, *Letters of St. Augustine* 102.34. Quoted in Phillip Cary, *Jonah*, Brazos Theological Commentary on the Bible (Grand Rapids: Brazos Press, 2008), 71.

> *In Judaism, the book of Jonah is the Haftorah for the afternoon of Yom Kippur. A "Haftorah" is an assigned reading from the Prophets that follows the Torah reading at each Sabbath celebration and on Jewish festivals and fast days. Yom Kippur is the day of national repentance and forgiveness in Judaism. Why Jonah? Because it speaks to God's willingness to forgive anyone who is willing to repent.*

write the message of the book of Jonah off as a late and evolved creation of a post-exilic author. Rather, we find ourselves (in the midst of our own narrow biases) being challenged with the same message as eighth-century Israel—to move out of our comfort zone and embrace God's global vision for this world he created. So this is our goal for this study—to take the message of this book at face value, and listen for the voice of God. Why? So that Jesus will not have to say of us what he said of his own generation—that the Ninevites did better than us (see Matthew 12:41; Luke 11:32).

How Is This Going to Work?

If your group has already worked through an *Epic of Eden* study, you're already pros. If not, here's the plan. The study revolves around a DVD/downloaded set of seven, approximately half-hour studies with Dr. Sandy Richter. These are designed to be viewed during group time once per week. The second component is a study guide for each of your group members that includes three individual studies per week—these are to be done at home whenever it fits an individual's schedule. In addition, the study guide will include all of the biblical passages discussed in each study. The third component is a brief leader's guide designed to help the leader to structure the group time. (You'll find this on page 125.) The idea is that each member will be working at home at their own pace on the three weekly studies. Do as much or as little as your schedule permits. No pressure, really. Once per week your group will gather to view the filmed study, talk about the individual work from the week, and focus on some group discussion questions. Our recommendation is that you set apart the first gathering to simply meet each other, drink some coffee and have some snacks, get your books, watch the introductory video, and make sure everyone is clear on the plan. It might also be wise to set apart a final gathering to debrief, ask and answer final questions, and conclude your time as a group.

Got it? Got it! Let the adventure begin!

What Is a Prophet?

A Word from the Author

As we consider plunging into the well-known book of Jonah, we are dealing once again with the "Great Barrier" . . . the cultural and historical barrier that stands between us and them. How desperately we want to hear what God wants to say to us through Jonah, but we stand at a distance. When it comes to studying the Prophets, the distance is not only historical and cultural, it is literary as well. What *is* a prophetic book? Why are there so many of them in the Old Testament? How are they organized? These issues were transparent to the ancient Israelites, but they are a whole new realm for us.

Real Time and Space

Let's start with what the prophetic books are. The technical term for the books that have been identified by the community of faith (past and present) as belonging in the Old Testament is the word *canon*. Out of the many psalms and proverbs put to parchment, the histories written, and the oracles preached, the canon includes the pieces that the community of faith identify as inspired by God and therefore have the "authority of faith and practice" over the people of God. The Greek word *kanōn* derives from a word meaning "reed" or "bar" and came to mean "ruler" or "measuring stick"—the idea is that these books, and these alone, have been measured and found worthy of sacred status. The Protestant Christian canon of the Old Testament includes the same list of books as the Jewish canon, but organizes them differently. In the Protestant canon, the writing Prophets are gathered into one file folder and placed in their perceived chronological order. [See figure 1.]

Hebrew Bible	Protestant Christian Old Testament
The Law *(Torah)*: Genesis, Exodus, Leviticus, Numbers, Deuteronomy	**The Pentateuch:** Genesis, Exodus, Leviticus, Numbers, Deuteronomy
The Prophets *(Nevi'im)*: Joshua, Judges, 1 & 2 Samuel, 1 & 2 Kings, Isaiah, Jeremiah, Ezekiel, Hosea, Joel, Amos, Obadiah, **Jonah**, Micah, Nahum, Habakkuk, Zephaniah, Haggai, Zechariah, Malachi	**The Historical Books:** Joshua, Judges, Ruth, 1 & 2 Samuel, 1 & 2 Kings, 1 & 2 Chronicles, Ezra, Nehemiah, Esther
The Writings *(Ketuvim)*: Psalms, Proverbs, Job The Five Scrolls: Song of Songs, Ruth, Lamentations, Ecclesiastes, Esther Daniel, Ezra, Nehemiah, 1 & 2 Chronicles	**Poetry & Wisdom:** Job, Psalms, Proverbs, Ecclesiastes, Song of Solomon
	The Prophets: Isaiah, Jeremiah, Lamentations, Ezekiel, Daniel, Hosea, Joel, Amos, Obadiah, **Jonah**, Micah, Nahum, Habakkuk, Zephaniah, Haggai, Zechariah, Malachi

The Apocrypha:
A final collection of books sometimes included in the Bible is known as the Apocrypha. *Some of this collection is included in the Roman Catholic and Orthodox canons, but it was excluded from the Protestant and Jewish canons. The word itself means "secret" or "obscure," and the title comes from the fact that the authorship of the books is either unknown or considered spurious. These books include: Tobit, Judith, additions to the book of Esther, the Wisdom of Solomon, Ecclesiasticus (Wisdom of ben Sirach), Baruch, additions to the book of Daniel, 1 & 2 Maccabees.*

Figure 1.

Meet the Prophets

First Contact

If someone were to ask you to name three prophets found in the Bible, could you do it? Five? List the first ones that come to mind. Jot down two pieces of information (or passages) that you know about each of them.

Into the Book

Open up the table of contents of your Bible. If your Bible is like mine, the listing of the Old Testament Books takes up a single page. Scan through the titles of the books. If you dare, put a colored dot or dash or underline every book you think belongs to the Prophets. How many have you found? Are there some that are much longer than others?

- Now find the book of Jonah. Where does this book fall in the list? Why do you think Jonah's book was placed where it is?

- Now actually turn in your Bible to the book of Jonah. What is the page number of the opening chapter?

▪ Flip through the book. How many chapters are in it?

▪ Keep flipping until you reach the book of Micah. How many pages are there in the book of Micah? How many chapters?

▪ Keeping a bookmark at Jonah 1, go back to your table of contents and find the book of Isaiah. Go to that page. Flip through that book. How many chapters do you find there?

▪ Keep flipping pages until you hit the book of Jeremiah. How many chapters are there? Any ideas as to why these books are so vastly different in length?

▪ Now read the opening verse of the book of Jonah, the opening verse of the book of Isaiah, and the opening verse of the book of Micah. Write here what is common between the opening verses of each of these books.

▪ What do you notice about the opening of Jonah that differs from Isaiah and Micah?

Jonah	Isaiah	Micah
Now the word of the LORD came to Jonah the son of Amittai, saying, "Arise, go to Nineveh, that great city, and call out against it, for their evil has come up before me." [ESV]	The vision of Isaiah the son of Amoz, which he saw concerning Judah and Jerusalem in the days of Uzziah, Jotham, Ahaz, and Hezekiah, kings of Judah. [ESV]	The word of the LORD that came to Micah of Moresheth in the days of Jotham, Ahaz, and Hezekiah, kings of Judah, which he saw concerning Samaria and Jerusalem. [ESV]

Real People, Real Places, Real Faith

As we will learn in our first lesson, the books of the Prophets are not typi-cally biographies of the prophets themselves. Rather, they are collections of the prophets' sermons. Sometimes these sermons are the result of visions they have seen, experiences they have had, or a direct word they heard from God and have been commanded to speak. Each of the prophets was a *very* public figure. They spoke to the nation and most expressly to the king. Ultimately, their job was to confront the people of Israel when they were failing to keep their covenant with God. When Israel broke that covenant, the leaders of the nation were *supposed* to lead them back. When the leaders didn't, the prophet launched. And boy did he launch. Note that each of Jonah's contemporaries identifies their tenure as prophet by the kings under which they served. The book of Jonah is the exception. We hear nothing of Jonah's king(s) in the *book* of Jonah, rather we find out about Jonah's tenure via the book of Kings. This is Israel's national history. And in 2 Kings 14:23–29 we read that Jonah is a northern prophet, who ministered during the reign of one of the Northern Kingdom's most famous kings, Jeroboam II. Read that passage, and take a moment to find and circle Jonah's king on the following time line.

Our People, Our Places, Our Faith

Communities are complicated. Whether you are dealing with a family, a school system, a city, a state, or a nation. It seems that human communi-ties in this fallen world of ours are always a mixed bag of the good, the bad, and the ugly. In my younger years, I was a complete and committed idealist. I truly believed that good people were always good, bad people were always bad, and life came in black and white. As the years have gone by I've realized that there's an awful lot of gray out there. You can be privi-leged to have your kids enrolled in a *great* school system and still wind up with the one teacher left in the mix who is a miserable, bitter old woman who clearly wishes she were anywhere else but educating your precious

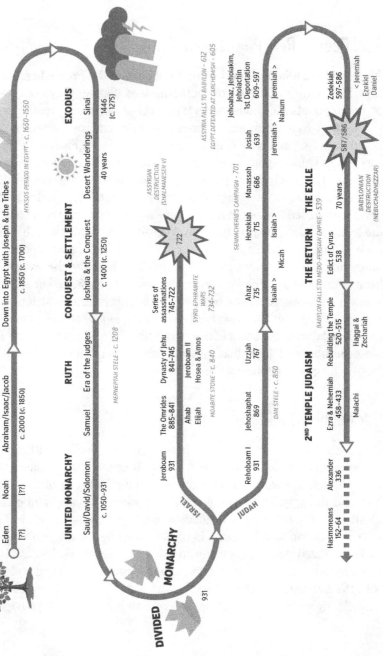

PATRIARCHAL PERIOD

Down into Egypt with Joseph & the Tribes

c. 1850 (c. 1700)

HYKSOS PERIOD IN EGYPT – c. 1650–1550

EXODUS

Sinai

1446
(c. 1275)

Desert Wanderings

40 years

CONQUEST & SETTLEMENT

Joshua & the Conquest

c. 1400 (c. 1250)

Abraham/Isaac/Jacob

c. 2000 (c. 1850)

Noah

[??]

Eden

[??]

RUTH

Era of the Judges

Samuel

UNITED MONARCHY

Saul/David/Solomon

c. 1050–931

MERNEPTAH STELE – c. 1208

Dynasty of Jehu
841–745

Jeroboam II
Hosea & Amos

The Omrides
885–841

Ahab
Elijah

Series of
assassinations
745–722

*SYRO-EPHRAIMITE
WARS
734–732*

*ASSYRIAN
DESTRUCTION
(SHALMANESER V)*

722

Jeroboam
931

Uzziah
767

Ahaz
735

Isaiah >

Micah

Jehoshaphat
869

MOABITE STONE – c. 840

DAM STELE – c. 850

Rehoboam I
931

ISRAEL

JUDAH

DIVIDED

MONARCHY

931

SENNACHERIB'S CAMPAIGN – 701

Hezekiah
715

Manasseh
686

Isaiah >

Josiah
639

Jeremiah >

Nahum

ASSYRIA FALLS TO BABYLON – 612
EGYPT DEFEATED AT CARCHEMISH – 605

Jehoahaz, Jehoiakim,
Jehoiachin
1st Deportation
609–597

Zedekiah
597–586

< Jeremiah
Ezekiel
Daniel

587/586

THE EXILE

*BABYLONIAN
DESTRUCTION
(NEBUCHADNEZZAR)*

70 years

THE RETURN

Edict of Cyrus
538

BABYLON FALLS TO MEDO-PERSIAN EMPIRE – 539

Rebuilding the Temple
520–515

Haggai &
Zechariah

2ND TEMPLE JUDAISM

Ezra & Nehemiah
458–433

Malachi

Alexander
336

Hasmoneans
152–64

All dates are BCE.

kindergartner. You can be a young professional paddling hard in the midst of the shark tank that you call your first job, knowing full well that the higher-ups are a hot mess, and in the midst of a desperate moment find out that there is one higher-up who is not only every inch an honest human being but totally goes to bat for you at great personal price. Equally, you can find yourself working for a Christian institution with a great reputation and find out that the folks who actually run the show are so turf-hungry that they will do anything to keep a good man (or a good idea) down. Or maybe you find yourself the citizen of a nation that is filled with dangerous ideals, self-serving politicians, graft and lies, and then out of the blue comes a Mr. Smith (that would be Jimmy Stewart's role in the 1939 *Mr. Smith Goes to Washington*), or an MLK, or an Elizabeth Warren (outspoken senior senator from Massachusetts), who, whatever their personal faults, totally puts themselves out there to make a difference.

And then you realize that David Mamet is wrong, old age and treachery will *not* always beat out youth and exuberance. And then tired and battle-scarred, you do it again—you take a stand. You tell yourself again that even in the midst of a system that seems completely broken *someone* has to be willing to make small moves against the darkness, even if it appears that their investment is doomed from the start.

Friends, this is what a prophet is. Are they always heard? Heck no. Do they pay a price for bucking the system? Absolutely. Are they written off as unrealistic hippy do-gooders or angry old/young men? Yes. Do they blow it themselves sometimes? Right there as well. But if justice and healing are ever going to see the light of day, we the people of God have got to be willing to live into the complexities of community with a commitment of *being* and *doing* right even when it hurts and we are vilified for it. Giving up is simply not an option.

The Authority of the Prophet

First Contact

Have you ever heard of an *orbuculum*? That is the technical word for a "crystal ball." How many times have you heard someone say, "If I had a crystal ball . . ." Considering the fact that folk as diverse as Diane Wood, Bob Kahn, and Michael Jordan have famous quotes citing the idiom, probably a bunch of times! As far as we know crystal balls were first utilized by the Celtic Druids, but gained so much influence over the centuries that during the Elizabethan period they were used to advise kings. Their function? To divine the future. To move human sight beyond its own finite limitations to see the other side. Hmmm . . . no wonder so many people seem to want one.

Into the Book

Today's study takes us into the book of Deuteronomy. Here we find the nation of Israel's legislation regarding the office of the prophet. And here we will find Yahweh's answer to the human desire for a crystal ball.

Deuteronomy 18:9–22

⁹When you enter the land the LORD your God is giving you, do not learn to imitate the detestable ways of the nations there. ¹⁰Let no one be found among you who sacrifices their son or daughter in the fire, who practices divination or sorcery, interprets omens, engages in witchcraft, ¹¹or casts spells, or who is a medium or spiritist or who consults the dead. ¹²Anyone who does these things is detestable to the LORD; because of these same detestable practices the LORD your God will drive out those nations before you. ¹³You must be blameless before the LORD your God.

¹⁴The nations you will dispossess listen to those who practice sorcery or divination. But as for you, the LORD your God has not permitted you to do so. ¹⁵The LORD your God will raise up for you a prophet like me from among you, from your fellow Israelites. You must listen to him. ¹⁶For this is what you asked of the LORD your God at Horeb on the day of the assembly when you said, "Let us not hear the voice of the LORD our God nor see this great fire anymore, or we will die."

¹⁷The LORD said to me: "What they say is good. ¹⁸I will raise up for them a prophet like you from among their fellow Israelites, and I will put my words in his mouth. He will tell them everything I command him. ¹⁹I myself will call to account anyone who does not listen to my words that the prophet speaks in my name. ²⁰But a prophet who presumes to speak in my name anything I have not commanded, or a prophet who speaks in the name of other gods, is to be put to death."

²¹You may say to yourselves, "How can we know when a message has not been spoken by the LORD?" ²²If what a prophet proclaims in the name of the LORD does not take place or come true, that is a message the LORD has not spoken. That prophet has spoken presumptuously, so do not be alarmed.

- Read verse 9 in several different versions if possible. How are the practices of the other nations described?

- In verses 10–14, underline the practices that the Israelites are *not* to imitate. (If you don't know what these words mean, take a quick look on Google.)

- In verses 15–20, whose words will be in the mouth of the prophet?

- Who do you think "me" is in verse 15?

- What will happen to those who do not pay attention to the words that the prophet speaks? Why is Yahweh so harsh about this command?

Real People, Real Places, Real Faith

Divine intermediaries, or mediators between the gods and humans, were well-known throughout the ancient Near East. As you'll hear in our video, people desperate to hear from the gods sought to communicate by means of omens (anything utilized to foreshadow the future). Omens could be observed in random events or actively solicited. A *random* event that may portend a future event could be something like an abnormal birth in the flock (a two-headed lamb, for instance). A *solicited* omen might be communication sought by means of "incubation" (sleeping in a holy site to obtain a holy dream) or extispicy (analyzing the entrails of a sacrificed animal), or astrology (observing the paths of the stars).

In the ancient world, kings would consult divine intermediaries regarding important decisions such as military campaigns, building projects, appointing civil servants, et cetera. The prophet Ezekiel alludes to this regarding the king of Babylon: "For the king of Babylon [Nebuchadnezzar] stands at the parting of the way, at the head of the two ways, to use divination; he shakes the arrows, he consults the household idols, he looks at the liver" (21:21 NASB). The story of the king of Moab hiring the local soothsayer

Balaam to read entrails on four mountains for a divination fee communicates similar methodology (see Numbers 22–23).

So obviously, seeking to hear from the gods by means of a dead animal's lungs and liver, shaking arrows, or reading the stars probably sounds very silly to us. But imagine *you* are one of those desperate souls needing a word from the gods and this is the only way you know how to get your god to speak. All of a sudden, rather than sounding silly, it now sounds very, very sad.

Our People, Our Places, Our Faith

In my many years of teaching and ministry, I have observed firsthand how desperately God's people want to hear from him. Over the years I've met hundreds at altars in camps and conferences, in my office or at a table in a café, who were asking for prayer, guidance, a word from their God. In today's study God promises Israel that he has no intention of concealing his will or requiring his people to *pay* someone else to find it for them. Instead, God promises that he will speak clearly to his people through his prophet. *And* the community of faith made sure that the most important of these words would be written down for subsequent generations. You and I are that subsequent generation, and our Bibles have preserved the words of the prophets for our guidance and our aid. As a result, there is *always* guidance for the believer in the Book. But there is also guidance for us through prayer. In this new covenant of ours, God has announced the impossible: that he has actually come to live within *every* believer (see Acts 2:1–4; Ephesians 2:19–22). *And* he has appointed leaders in this new covenant who can speak to us on his behalf (see 1 Corinthians 12:28–29). Moreover, we are told that "the word of God is alive and active. Sharper than any double-edged sword" (Heb. 4:12), and Jesus himself has become our advocate such that we can "approach God's throne of grace with confidence, so that we may receive mercy and find grace to help us in our time of need" (Heb. 4:16). In sum, in this new covenant, God actually *speaks* to the average, everyday believer and *we* can speak to him. So what is it you (the average, everyday believer) need to hear from God today? Why don't you pause now and tell him?

DAY THREE

The Prophet before Yahweh's Divine Council

First Contact

Have you ever seen a preacher (either live or on TV) claim to know something God was speaking to someone else? Did you have confidence in that preacher's claim? Why or why not?

Into the Book

In yesterday's study you read about divine intermediaries. Today we are with Isaiah as he encounters Yahweh's divine council and receives his commission to become a divine intermediary. We'll read the same story involving a certain Micaiah ben Imlah. And we are very interested in the fact that in Yahweh's government each of these encounters looks very different from what we might find in Canaanite religion.

Isaiah Isaiah 6:1–8 (NASB)	Micaiah ben Imlah 1 Kings 22:19–23, 28 (NASB)
¹In the year of King Uzziah's death I saw the Lord sitting on a throne, lofty and exalted, with the train of His robe filling the temple. ²Seraphim stood above Him, each having six wings: with two he covered his face, and with two he covered his feet, and with two he flew. ³And one called out to another and said, "Holy, Holy, Holy, is the LORD of hosts, The whole earth is full of His glory." ⁴And the foundations of the thresholds trembled at the voice of him who called out, while the temple was filling with smoke. ⁵Then I said, "Woe is me, for I am ruined! Because I am a man of unclean lips, And I live among a people of unclean lips; For my eyes have seen the King, the LORD of hosts." ⁶Then one of the seraphim flew to me with a burning coal in his hand, which he had taken from the altar with tongs. ⁷He touched my mouth with it and said, "Behold, this has touched your lips; and your iniquity is taken away and your sin is forgiven." ⁸Then I heard the voice of the Lord, saying, "Whom shall I send, and who will go for Us?" Then I said, "Here am I. Send me!"	¹⁹Micaiah said, "Therefore, hear the word of the LORD. I saw the LORD sitting on His throne, and all the host of heaven standing by Him on His right and on His left. ²⁰The LORD said, 'Who will entice Ahab to go up and fall at Ramoth-gilead?' And one said this while another said that. ²¹Then a spirit came forward and stood before the LORD and said, 'I will entice him.' ²²The LORD said to him, 'How?' And he said, 'I will go out and be a deceiving spirit in the mouth of all his prophets.' Then He said, 'You are to entice him and also prevail. Go and do so.' ²³Now therefore, behold, the LORD has put a deceiving spirit in the mouth of all these your prophets; and the LORD has proclaimed disaster against you." ²⁸Micaiah said, "If you indeed return safely the LORD has not spoken by me." And he said, "Listen, all you people."

Isaiah Isaiah 6:1–8 (NASB)	Micaiah ben Imlah 1 Kings 22:19–23, 28 (NASB)
What does Isaiah see and hear?	What does Micaiah see and hear?
What setting is described here? Where is Isaiah?	What setting is Micaiah describing?
What is Isaiah's response to what/who he sees?	What is Micaiah's response to what he witnesses?
Why do you think the seraph touches Isaiah's mouth?	Go back to the Deuteronomy passage you read on Day Two of this week and re-read especially verses 17–22. What similarity do you find in Micaiah's words?
What is Isaiah's response to Yahweh's call?	

Real People, Real Places, Real Faith

In the Canaanite divine council, the more powerful gods would argue out their plans for humanity in a free-for-all that involved debate, passion, and more than a bit of manipulation until a final ruling surfaced. In my classes I often compare this scene to a discussion on gun control at a family holiday meal. After the decision was made, for good or for ill, it was always the lowest-ranking god at the table who got the job of announcing the news to humanity.

In Yahweh's divine council this was *not* the case. There was no argument, no debate, no one-upmanship. Rather, Yahweh consulted his council and then made the decision himself (this would be the difference between monotheism and polytheism). And rather than a low-ranking deity being sent as the messenger of the gods, here the *human* prophet, who had been caught up into the very presence of the divine council, who had heard the ruling with his very own ears, was commissioned to bring God's word to God's people. This was the ultimate source of the prophet's authority. The prophet was a divine emissary, not simply a human with a great sermon. He spoke on God's behalf as a diplomat communicates the will of his or her president. The populace ignored this message at their own peril.

Our People, Our Places, Our Faith

Read Psalm 119:33–48 out loud. Let the words rest on you. Can you hear this author's hunger for the Word of God? Can you hear how the psalmist is *completely* convinced that the Word of God is his best hope and only defense against the vagaries of this world? This entire psalm, the longest in your Bible (176 verses!) recites in elegant poetic verse the believer's deepest need—the Word of God.

Do you share a fraction of the psalmist's conviction that the Word of God is the answer to your need? If not, ask the Holy Spirit who dwells within you to convince you of that truth. And pray for me while you're at it.

The Cast of Characters

Jonah, Gath-hepher, and Jeroboam II versus the Nation of Assyria and the City of Nineveh

A Word from the Author

As for the prophets, they of all the Old Testament characters could explain to us the work of the Holy Spirit. For Isaiah, Jeremiah, Micaiah ben Imlah, Amos, and Ezekiel all tell us the same tale. Upon their commission, each is caught up into the royal throne room of God, each overhears the deliberations of his divine council, and each receives their commission to speak on his behalf (Isa. 6:1–6; Jer. 23:16–22; 1 Kings 22:19–23; Ezek. 1:1–2:7; Amos 3:7). Indeed, Jeremiah gives voice to Yahweh's lament.

But if they [the false prophets] had stood in my council, they would have proclaimed my words to my people. (Jer. 23:22)

Each of these is "raised up" by the power of the Holy Spirit and, as promised in Deuteronomy 18:18, becomes the mouthpiece of God.*

Real Time and Space

In the first half of the eighth century (800–750 BCE) the Divided Kingdom was ruled by Jeroboam II in the north (Israel), and Jehoshaphat of Judah in the south. Both of these kings were strong leaders and established a level of cooperation with each other and their neighbors such that they were able to control the critical trade routes connecting their territories to Egypt and to the East. The result was exceptional economic prosperity for both countries. Thinking back to the complexities of community, it is one of the ironies of the biblical story that the forty-one-year reign of Jeroboam II stands as the high watermark for the Northern Kingdom economically and militarily. This king is condemned by the historian as rebellious and wicked, and the prophets Hosea and Amos repeatedly decry his pitiless abuse of the voiceless in Israel. But even so, Jeroboam II was the most politically successful king in the history of the Northern Kingdom.

The Assyrian Empire (east of Israel) was one of the ancient superpowers in Israel's world. It began its initial rise to power in 1075 BCE and continued to be a major player until its demise at the hands of the Babylonians in 612 BCE. The Assyrians were the warrior kings of the ancient world, the powerhouse of the Fertile Crescent. Everyone heard their names and trembled. As we will study, brutality and oppression were the hallmarks of their rule. These folks celebrated the torture and execution of their foes in text and image, they created the idea of exile, they crippled anyone who would rise in opposition. Their goal? To rule the world, of course.

---

*Sandra Richter, eds. J. W. Bareau and B. F. Jones, "What Do I Know of Holy?" *Spirit of God: Christian Renewal in the Community of Faith* (Wheaton, IL: InterVarsity Press, 2015), 31–32.

Of great interest to us is the fact that this ambition was interrupted by a "brief eclipse"* in Assyrian power in the first half of the eighth century. This eclipse allowed some of the smaller players in the ancient Near East to expand their influence and land holdings. And as you have probably guessed by now, the first half of the eighth century was when Jeroboam II and Jehoshaphat ruled our Divided Kingdom. In 745 BCE Tiglath-Pileser III seized the Assyrian throne, and resurrected the Neo-Assyrian Empire—and in 738 BCE the military machine of Assyria once again set its sights on the West.

---

*A. K. Grayson, "Assryia, Assyrians," *Dictionary of the Old Testament: Historical Books* (Wheaton IL: InterVarsity Press, 2005), 100.

Jonah

First Contact

Have you ever been in a setting where someone thought you were irreparably naïve for assuming that a biblical narrative or figure was an actual *person*? I sure have. What sort of evidence do you think the average skeptic would need to convince them that Jonah (our popular legend) was a real person who lived in real space and time? What sort of evidence would you need?

Into the Book

Take a look back at Week One, Day One. What was it that was different about the opening verses of Jonah as compared to Isaiah and Micah? Today's study will fill in those blanks. Our reading is found in 2 Kings, which is part of what scholars call the national history of Israel. In other words, it is an ancient, intentional effort at history writing.

2 Kings 14:23-26

²³In the fifteenth year of Amaziah the son of Joash, king of Judah, Jeroboam the son of Joash, king of Israel, began to reign in Samaria, and he reigned forty-one years. ²⁴And he did what was evil in the sight of the LORD. He did not depart from all the sins of Jeroboam the son of Nebat, which he made Israel to sin. ²⁵He restored the border of Israel from Lebo-hamath as far as the Sea of the Arabah, according to the word of the LORD, the God of Israel, which he spoke by his servant Jonah the son of Amittai, the prophet, who was from Gath-hepher. ²⁶For the LORD saw that the affliction of Israel was very bitter, for there was none left, bond or free, and there was none to help Israel. (ESV)

- Underline the names of each of the people mentioned.

- Who is Amaziah the son of Joash and where does he rule?

- Who is Jeroboam the son of Joash and where does he rule? Find him on your time line. (Hint: this is Jeroboam II.)

- Circle the things that Jeroboam the son of Joash did during his reign.

- Who is the other Jeroboam, the son of Nebat? Find him on your time line. (Hint: this is Jeroboam I. If you need a reminder about this Jeroboam and his sins, read 1 Kings 12:25–33.)

- Who is Jonah the son of Amittai? Now re-read Jonah 1:1. If Jonah the son of Amittai is listed in the national history in 2 Kings, what does that tell us about the original audience's view of his historicity?

- Find Hamath and the Sea of the Arabah (the Dead Sea) on the map titled "The Assyrian Empire" in your pullout. Any ideas why reestablishing Israel's boundaries from Hamath to the Dead Sea might be significant to the Northern Kingdom's economy?

■ Find Gath-hepher on the map titled "The Divided Kingdom."

Real People, Real Places, Real Faith

Often it is hard for us to think of the people in the Bible as *real* people. Pause over the fact that Jonah is recorded to have had a *career* in Jeroboam II's kingdom. Pause over Jonah's identity as a public figure that was known broadly enough to be associated with a critical military victory in Israel's national history. This sort of blows us off our flannel boards, if you get my drift. Perhaps more important is the fact that although Jonah must have said and done *many* things in the course his career, the only aspect of his prophetic ministry that made the cut (and thereby winds up in our Bible) is this one story. No oracles, no other narratives, just this one chapter of his story: a prophet, a great fish, and the Ninevites. What do you think this tells us about this one episode in our prophet's life?

Our People, Our Places, Our Faith

The materials collected in the biblical text were preserved for the sake of future generations. In other words, for *us*. The book of Jonah, and the Bible as a whole, were not simply preserved for the sake of maintaining antiquities or recording history. Rather, these materials were preserved to *teach* future generations about the mighty acts of God and his current ambitions for his people. Out of all that Jonah ever said and did, it was *this* story that the Holy Spirit deemed necessary for our formation as the people of God. You know the story. Or at least you think you do. And you now know that Jonah's book wound up included in the Minor Prophets. Why do you think God made sure *this* story wound up in *your* Bible?

Assyria

First Contact

As a Star Trek devotee, for decades I found an apt illustration for the Assyrian Empire in the Borg of the television series *The Next Generation*. The classic quote for this terrifying collective of cybernetic organisms? "Resistance is futile; you will be assimilated." But, alas, time marches on and students get younger every year. So now there are very few who have any idea who Jean-Luc Picard was or *even* James T. Kirk. (Can you imagine?!) And so my illustration has lost its punch. But now, unfortunately, I have a new one. A group whose ambition is to conquer the world. A group whose strategy is to terrify and brutalize. A force who portrays themselves in word and image as a constant threat to anyone who resists them, who are more terrifying than your worst nightmare. If you don't know who I'm speaking of, check it out on YouTube. Their name is ISIS.

Into the Book

As mentioned in the Real Time and Space section at the beginning of this week's study, the Assyrian Empire regularly

Israel = Northern Kingdom
Judah = Southern Kingdom
Samaria = Capital of the
northern kingdom of Israel

occupied the nightmares of the kings of the Fertile Crescent. And with the birth of the Neo-Assyrian Empire in the second half of the eighth century, Israel and Judah's fates would be directly tied to those of Neo-Assyria until the Babylonians arrived on the scene in 612 BCE. In today's readings, we'll look at a few examples of Israel and Judah's interactions with the Assyrians. Our goal is to attempt to step into their real space and time. As you read these passages, remember that we're talking about *real* people, who—like us—are afraid of their national enemies, and whose greatest goal is to simply keep their homes and children safe against the dangers of this world

Choose two of the following four passages to read. Underline the names of the kings of Israel and circle the names of the Assyrian kings. Highlight what you learn about Israel's interactions with Assyria.

2 Kings 15:17-20

¹⁷In the thirty-ninth year of Azariah king of Judah, Menahem son of Gadi became king of Israel, and he reigned in Samaria ten years. ¹⁸He did evil in the eyes of the LORD. During his entire reign he did not turn away from the sins of Jeroboam son of Nebat, which he had caused Israel to commit.

¹⁹Then Pul king of Assyria invaded the land, and Menahem gave him a thousand talents of silver to gain his support and strengthen his own hold on the kingdom. ²⁰Menahem exacted this money from Israel. Every wealthy person had to contribute fifty shekels of silver to be given to the king of Assyria. So the king of Assyria withdrew and stayed in the land no longer.

> ■ In the days of Menahem, bits and pieces of silver operated as "money" (*hacksilber*). There was no coinage yet, but weighed silver functioned in the same fashion. According to John Holladay, an equivalent number in the US economy for what Assyria asked of King Menahem was $47,114, 969!* If you were a citizen of

---

*See Sandra Richter, "The Question of Provenance and the Economies of Deuteronomy" in *Journal for the Study of the Old Testament* 42.1 (2017): 31–35.

Menahem's kingdom, how would you feel about his new emergency tax to pay off such an enormous sum?

- How do you think Menahem went about collecting all the silver bullion from his people so quickly?

2 Kings 16:5-9

⁵Then Rezin king of Aram and Pekah son of Remaliah king of Israel marched up to fight against Jerusalem and besieged Ahaz [king of Judah], but they could not overpower him. ⁶At that time, Rezin king of Aram recovered Elath for Aram by driving out the people of Judah. Edomites then moved into Elath and have lived there to this day.

⁷Ahaz sent messengers to say to Tiglath-Pileser king of Assyria, "I am your servant and vassal. Come up and save me out of the hand of the king of Aram and of the king of Israel, who are attacking me." ⁸And Ahaz took the silver and gold found in the temple of the LORD and in the treasuries of the royal palace and sent it as a gift to the king of Assyria. ⁹The king of Assyria complied by attacking Damascus and capturing it. He deported its inhabitants to Kir and put Rezin to death.

- At this point you know all about Tiglath-Pileser of Assyria. What was he famous for and when?

- If you've done *The Epic of Eden: Isaiah* study, you know all about Ahaz. Was he a good king or a bad king?

- When Ahaz said, "I am your servant," in the language of treaty-speak (*The Epic of Eden: Understanding the Old Testament*), what was he saying?

- Why in the world would Ahaz ask Tiglath-Pileser for help?

■ How did Ahaz sweeten the pot to get Tiglath-Pileser to help him?

■ Where did Ahaz get his silver and gold bullion to pay off the king of Assyria? Does this sound like a regular withdrawal from the bank or emergency measures?

2 Kings 18:9-12

⁹In the fourth year of King Hezekiah, which was the seventh year of Hoshea son of Elah, king of Israel, Shalmaneser king of Assyria came up against Samaria and besieged it, ¹⁰and at the end of three years he took it. In the sixth year of Hezekiah, which was the ninth year of Hoshea king of Israel, Samaria was taken. ¹¹The king of Assyria carried the Israelites away to Assyria and put them in Halah, and on the Habor, the river of Gozan, and in the cities of the Medes, ¹²because they did not obey the voice of the LORD their God but transgressed his covenant, even all that Moses the servant of the LORD commanded. They neither listened nor obeyed. (ESV)

■ Do we know what the city of Samaria is to the Northern Kingdom? Why is it significant that the Assyrians besieged Samaria?

■ What do you think the quality of life was like inside the city walls of Samaria after three years of siege?

■ Can you use Google to find Halah, Habor, and Gozan?

■ We stated earlier that the Assyrians actually created the military strategy of exile. To exile a population is to cart off an entire nation as a refugee community and relocate them. List three things here that you know about refugees and relocation camps. (Please feel free to include your own experiences.)

2 Kings 18:13-16

¹³In the fourteenth year of King Hezekiah, Sennacherib king of Assyria came up against all the fortified cities of Judah and took them. ¹⁴And Hezekiah king of Judah sent to the king of Assyria at Lachish, saying, "I have done wrong; withdraw from me. Whatever you impose on me I will bear." And the king of Assyria required of Hezekiah king of Judah three hundred talents of silver and thirty talents of gold. ¹⁵And Hezekiah gave him all the silver that was found in the house of the LORD and in the treasuries of the king's house. ¹⁶At that time Hezekiah stripped the gold from the doors of the temple of the LORD and from the doorposts that Hezekiah king of Judah had overlaid and gave it to the king of Assyria. (ESV)

- For those who've worked through *The Epic of Eden: Isaiah*, you know all about King Hezekiah, his courage in resisting Sennacherib, and ultimately what happened to Lachish. For those in your group who've done this study,

  - Was Hezekiah a good king or a bad king?

  - Which prophet told Hezekiah to stand his ground?

  - What was going to happen to Lachish?

- According to John Holladay, the amount of tribute Hezekiah paid is equivalent to $49,000,087 in US currency.* Again, does this sound like standard taxation and withdrawals from the royal coffers, or something else?

---

*See Sandra Richter, "The Question of Provenance and the Economics of Deuteronomy," *Journal for the Study of the Old Testament* 42.1 (2017): 23–50.

Real People, Real Places, Real Faith

As we've alluded to, in 745 BCE the tables will turn in the ancient Near East. Whereas Assyria had been experiencing a dark age of sorts in the first half of the eighth century—a brief eclipse that had allowed for the blossoming of Jeroboam II's kingdom—in 745 BCE Tiglath-Pileser III would seize Assyria's throne and birth the Neo-Assyrian Empire. He would completely reorganize his nation as a military state, establish the first fully professional standing army of the ancient world, and set about reestablishing Assyria as the Borg of the ancient Near East.

> The result was constant military activity throughout his reign, and over-flowing coffers at home. For those in the path of expansion who chose to cooperate with the crown, a vassal relationship with Assyria was initiated. . . . For those less cooperative, the local leader was stripped of his office (often executed) and replaced with a man of the emperor's choosing. For those least cooperative, local government was obliterated, an Assyrian governor established, and the territory absorbed into the empire as a province. This final stage saw exile—a strategy designed to strip the conquered nation of its will to rebel by relocating the bulk of its population elsewhere. In this fashion, national identity was lost, dissident factions dissolved, and the new heterogeneous populace in both the old and new territories were left with survival as their only objective and Assyria as their only lord. As attested by every epigraphic and visual resource available to us, the Neo-Assyrian Empire celebrated and propagated its reputation for unprecedented brutality. Their goal was to instill a level of terror that intimidated its opponents into early submission, and a level of demolition that stripped its conquered foes of the agency to ever rise in defiance again. And although Assyria perhaps did not initially intend to absorb these foreign territories into the empire, the end result was full assimilation.[*]

[*]Sandra Richter, eds. Bill T. Arnold and Richard S. Hess, "Eighth Century Issues: The World of Jeroboam II, the Fall of Samaria, and the Reign of Hezekiah," in *Ancient Israel's History: An Introduction to Issues and Sources* (Grand Rapids, MI: Baker Academic, 2014), 337–38.

Our People, Our Places, Our Faith

Now that you know a bit about the ancient nation of Assyria, how would you describe them in modern terms? If they existed in contemporary times, what nation might you associate them with? Can you feel some of Jonah's emotion when he is called to go share the gospel with these people? How would you react if tomorrow morning in your private devotion time God asked you to do something similar?

Nineveh

First Contact

Can you think of one place in the world that you would avoid at all costs? Narrow that to one city—perhaps Caracas, Baghdad, Las Vegas, New York City, Johannesburg, New Orleans, or Pyongyang? What about that city would make you avoid it?

Into the Book

We first read about the city of Nineveh in the book of Genesis where the author tells us that the descendants of Noah's son Ham built the city of Nineveh in Assyria (see Genesis 10:1–12). In the opening verses of the book of Jonah, we read God's instructions to Jonah to go to Nineveh. In today's study, we will explore what we know about this city from the biblical text.

Read the following verses and underline any descriptions you find about the city of Nineveh.

Jonah 1:2

²"Go to the great city of Nineveh and preach against it, because its wicked-ness has come up before me."

Jonah 3:1-3

¹Then the word of the Lᴏʀᴅ came to Jonah a second time: ²"Go to the great city of Nineveh and proclaim to it the message I give you."

³Jonah obeyed the word of the Lᴏʀᴅ and went to Nineveh. Now Nineveh was a very large city; it took three days to go through it.

Jonah 4:11

¹¹"And should I [the Lᴏʀᴅ] not have concern for the great city of Nineveh, in which there are more than a hundred and twenty thousand people who cannot tell their right hand from their left—and also many animals?"

Real People, Real Places, Real Faith

In the days of Jonah, Nineveh was one of the oldest and most venerated cities in Mesopotamia—enormous, fortified, and recognized by all as a royal city. Michael Roaf speaks of it as "the natural center of Assyria." Surrounded by excellent farm land, lying on an important crossing of the Tigris, and graced with the chief temple of the Assyrian goddess of love and war, Ishtar, Nineveh had always been influential . . . even before it became the capital. Archaeology has demonstrated that the perimeter of the great wall surrounding the 1800-acre site was about 7.5 miles long, and most unique is that the Khawṣar River flowed through the center of the city to join the Tigris on the western side. Within fifty years, Nineveh would become the capital of the reemerging Assyrian Empire under Sennacherib, who constructed his famous "palace without a rival" (600 by 630 feet, with at least 80 rooms) at its center. Ashurbanipal later constructed his infamous library in the city as well.*

But in Jonah's day, from the death of Assyrian Adad-nirari III in 782 BCE until the ascendancy of Tiglath-Pileser III in 745 BCE, the *nation* of Assyria was in trouble. Practically paralyzed by an ongoing life-and-death struggle with the mountain tribes of Urartu (and Mannai and Madai), who had managed to press their advantage to within one hundred miles of Nineveh, Assyria also experienced a dramatic solar eclipse on June 15, 763 BCE, along with famine in 765 BCE and 763 BCE. The result was a profound sense of their own vulnerability. And in the minds of many commentators, this sense of vulnerability is a compelling backdrop for the success of Jonah's preaching.

In contrast, these same years were the Northern Kingdom's best. Israel reached the apex of its influence and wealth in the first half of the eighth century. Jeroboam II stretched Israel's boundaries to their farthest limits, and archaeology attests to his ivory-embellished capital city and flourishing trade economy. As we will rehearse before we are done with this study, the tables would turn dramatically in 745 BCE. With the ascendancy of Tiglath-Pileser III in Assyria, Israel and Judah would "witness a power shift in the international scene that will alter the face of world history."** The birth of the Neo-Assyrian Empire literally changed the world. And due to its strategic position along the crossroads of the international highways, the Northern Kingdom would be one of the first victims of its expanding boundaries.

---

*Michael Roaf, *Cultural Atlas of Mesopotamia and the Ancient Near East* (Oxford Press, 1990), 182, 186.

**Sandra Richter, eds. Bill T. Arnold and Richard S. Hess, "Eighth-Century Issues: The World of Jeroboam II, the Fall of Samaria, and the Reign of Hezekiah," in *Ancient Israel's History: An Introduction to Issues and Sources* (Grand Rapids, MI: Baker Academic, 2014), 336.

Our People, Our Places, Our Faith

Have you ever heard of Jim Elliot? Perhaps his wife, Elisabeth Elliot? These folks are renowned for their commitment to missions. While serving as young missionaries in Ecuador in the 1950s, Jim and Elisabeth, along with four other missionaries, attempted to reach out to a people group known as the Auca Indians (now known as the Huaorani/Waorani tribe)—a group that no outsider had been able to engage with the gospel and live to tell the tale. After a successful attempt at communicating with one of the tribe's men, the young missionaries were encouraged and the men made plans to visit the Huaorani people again. Upon their arrival this second time, however, our heroes were met with spears and all five men were savagely murdered. Elisabeth Elliot, Jim's young widow, with their not-yet-one-year-old daughter made the incredible decision to remain in Ecuador and try again. With the help of some of the indigenous women, Elisabeth and her colleague Rachel Saint succeeded where the men had failed. They learned the Huaorani language, and in October 1958, Mrs. Elliot went to live with the Huaorani with her now three-year-old child. If there ever was a missionary who had a reason to fear and hate their target audience, I think Elisabeth Elliot qualifies. Where does someone get that kind of courage? What sort of love do you think drove Elisabeth and Rachel to return to the Huaorani?

To Hurl or Not to Hurl

A Word from the Author

In the very first verses of our book we read that God commanded Jonah to go to Nineveh to tell his enemies about his God. In his fear and his (well-earned) hatred of the Assyrians, Jonah instead ran the other way. As we learned in our own study here and in lecture, it is likely that you and I might have responded in exactly the same way. But there is something built into Jonah's response that might not be obvious to us—Jonah, the right-reverend holy man, apparently thought in some small part of his soul that Yahweh's authority was limited to the land of Israel. As you will learn, this is indeed just what any of his neighboring pagan friends would think. In the ancient Near East, it was assumed that deities were limited to their territories, and if a neighboring king was able to defeat your army it was because that king's god was bigger and better than your god (kind of like quarterbacks and the NFL). Now Jonah, of course, knew better than to think Yahweh's authority only extended to the borders of Israel; he even stated such when questioned. But when he was afraid, really afraid, he defaulted to the worldview of his culture instead of his faith. That is something we need to think about. When we are afraid, really afraid, what is our default worldview?

Real Time and Space

So far we have learned that Jonah was a prophet in the northern kingdom of Israel whom Yahweh commanded to go to Nineveh, one of the imperial cities of the nation of Assyria. In order to understand exactly what was happening in the beginning verses of the book of Jonah, we need to turn once again to our maps. Pull out your insert and find the map of the ancient Near East. The places that we're interested in are Israel, Nineveh, Joppa, and Tarshish. Notice where Nineveh is located—several hundred miles to the north and east of Israel.

Our author tells us that Jonah "went down to Joppa and found a ship going to Tarshish" in an effort to flee from "the presence of the Lord" (1:3 NRSV). Joppa, modern-day Jaffa, located on the Mediterranean coast, was the main port city of Israel in Jonah's day. From here, Jonah boarded a ship heading for Tarshish, most likely the Phoenician port city of Tartessus in southwestern Spain—two thousand miles west of Israel! And although Tarshish was a well-known destination for international maritime trade (see 1 Kings 10:22; 22:48; Isaiah 23:1), it was also a heck of a long way away. Hence, our prophet gets on a trade ship thinking that he can somehow conceal himself from the presence of Yahweh by hiding among the cargo. But Yahweh knows where his servant is and where Jonah is going, and he's going to go get him.

The Cargo

First Contact

When you hear the term "free port," what comes to mind? Panama? Shanghai? An innovative business venture built upon a port open to all traders where goods are exempt from customs duty and scrutiny? Or do you think of desperate characters who will work any job for the right price, and questionable cargo that is best not identified? History and experience tell us a free port is both.

Into the Book

We know from Jonah 1:3 that the ship that Jonah boarded was a cargo ship carrying goods to Tarshish. The text does not state what those goods were, but we can get an idea of some types of cargo that were delivered by sea during the days of Solomon. In addition, the prophets Ezekiel and Jeremiah also tell us what items were traded at Tarshish.

Read the following passages and highlight those items that were transported by sea.

1 Kings 5:1-6, 10-11

[1]Now Hiram king of Tyre sent his servants to Solomon when he heard that they had anointed him king in place of his father, for Hiram always loved David. [2]And Solomon sent word to Hiram, [3]"You know that David my father could not build a house for the name of the LORD his God because of the warfare with which his enemies surrounded him, until the LORD put them under the soles of his feet. [4]But now the LORD my God has given me rest on every side. There is neither adversary nor misfortune. [5]And so I intend to build a house for the name of the LORD my God, as the LORD said to David my father, 'Your son, whom I will set on your throne in your place, shall build the house for my name.' [6]Now therefore command that cedars of Lebanon be cut for me. And my servants will join your servants, and I will pay you for your servants such wages as you set, for you know that there is no one among us who knows how to cut timber like the Sidonians.". . .

[10]So Hiram supplied Solomon with all the timber of cedar and cypress that he desired, [11]while Solomon gave Hiram 20,000 cors of wheat as food for his household, and 20,000 cors of beaten oil. Solomon gave this to Hiram year by year. (ESV)

1 Kings 9:26-28

[26]King Solomon built a fleet of ships at Ezion-geber, which is near Eloth on the shore of the Red Sea, in the land of Edom. [27]And Hiram sent with the fleet his servants, seamen who were familiar with the sea, together with the servants of Solomon. [28]And they went to Ophir and brought from there gold, 420 talents, and they brought it to King Solomon. (ESV)

1 Kings 22:48a

[48]Jehoshaphat made ships of Tarshish to go to Ophir for gold. . . . (ESV)

2 Chronicles 9:21

²¹For the king's ships went to Tarshish with the servants of Hiram. Once every three years the ships of Tarshish used to come bringing gold, silver, ivory, apes, and peacocks. (ESV)

Ezekiel 27:12, 18–19

¹²"Tarshish did business with you [Tyre] because of your great wealth of every kind; silver, iron, tin, and lead they exchanged for your wares. . . . ¹⁸Damascus did business with you for your abundant goods, because of your great wealth of every kind; wine of Helbon and wool of Sahar ¹⁹and casks of wine from Uzal they exchanged for your wares; wrought iron, cassia, and calamus were bartered for your merchandise. (ESV)

Jeremiah 10:9a

⁹Beaten silver is brought from Tarshish, and gold from Uphaz. (ESV)

Real People, Real Places, Real Faith

As you will hear in the lecture, in 1999 during a deep-sea expedition off the coast of Ashkelon, Robert Ballard and Lawrence Stager discovered two sunken Phoenician ships. These ships, dated somewhere between 750 and 700 BCE, measured about fifty-two feet long and about twenty feet wide. These ships and others like them are extremely important to archaeology because shipwrecks are hard to loot, and the cargo in their hulls tells us who is trading what to whom and in what quantities. The cargo of these particular ships included large storage jars full of wine with each ship transporting more than twelve tons of wine! As our knowledge of the economies of the Fertile Crescent expands, we now realize that Israel and its neighbors were heavily involved in high-stakes trade that transported caravan treasures off the desert, and moved them by ship to the farthest reaches of their known world. Gold, silver, iron, cedar, almug, ebony, ivory, copper, jewels, apes, the pelts of exotic animals, and African slaves are named as cargo items. The crews and captains who sailed these ships were the sorts of people who asked only one question: "How much?" So for one provincial Israelite academic from the backwoods of Gath-hepher in Zebulun to head to the docks with money to spare for his fare . . . well, he could go just about anywhere he wanted, and no one would have any interest in asking him why.

Our People, Our Places, Our Faith

The obvious question that this part of Jonah's story asks each of us is: Have you ever found yourself in circumstances where your only thought was to hide from what you knew God had told you to do? Have you found yourself dodging a calling that was insistently whispered in your soul because the financial feasibility was simply impossible? Or perhaps on a board of elders where you knew your opinion was unpopular, but right all the same? Or in a meeting where you *knew* that an honest woman would take a stand? As I've told my undergrads more than once, it doesn't matter what vocation you choose, you will always find yourself in a position where your faith demands that you have to swim against the current. Sometimes that calling will require a yes when everything rational says no. Sometimes that calling will require a no when everyone around you is saying yes. It won't be easy. But easy isn't the Christian life.

The Polytheists

First Contact

My friend and coauthor Kathy Noftsinger related the following story to me about an encounter she had on one of her many international travels, this time to India.

> This was only my third time traveling overseas and I wasn't quite prepared for the culture shock I experienced. The deluge of temples with their statues to the hundreds (some say millions) of gods of Hinduism was particularly daunting. I vividly recall the stench of the temples—filled with rotting food, animal dung, and blood. And I will never forget the enormous (and a bit terrifying) statue of Hanuman, the monkey god. Hanuman towered over buildings and trees with his pale white skin, black eyes, and elaborate golden headdress. One look at him (combined with the ever-present stench) made me feel super uncomfortable and even a bit nauseated. One in our party turned to a well-educated Indian woman who we met during out time in her country and asked her to help us understand how one could think in terms of worshipping so many gods. She asked us a question I will never forget, "With millions of gods, how do we know which one is the right one? So we pray to them all."

Into the Book

There is a lot of action in the next few verses of Jonah. We are particularly interested in the verb "to hurl," as all the characters hurl something somewhere. And, of course, this sort of literary repetition should catch our attention as readers. As you read, pay attention to the verbs and who is performing the action. We are particularly interested in the actions of the sailors and the captain and the belief system that stands behind their actions.

Jonah 1:4-6

⁴But the LORD *hurled* a great wind upon the sea, and there was a mighty tempest on the sea, so that the ship threatened to break up. ⁵Then the mariners were afraid, and each cried out to his god. And they *hurled* the cargo that was in the ship into the sea to lighten it for them. But Jonah had gone down into the inner part of the ship and had lain down and was fast asleep. ⁶So the captain came and said to him, "What do you mean, you sleeper? Arise, call out to your god! Perhaps the god will give a thought to us, that we may not perish." (ESV, emphasis added)

■ Complete the following chart.

What Yahweh did and why?	What the mariners did and why?	What Jonah did and why?	What the captain did and why?

- What images does the word *hurl* bring to your mind? What types of things does a person typically hurl?

- What do the phrases "each cried out to his god" and "call out to your god" indicate about the characters' belief systems and their emotions?

- Do you find it ironic that the captain doesn't seem to care *who* Jonah's god is, just that he starts praying, *now*?

Real People, Real Places, Real Faith

Simply defined, "polytheism" is the worship of many gods (as opposed to the worship of *one* god, "monotheism"). A polytheist believes that there is an array of gods who are in regular conflict over the control of the universe—which, of course, makes it very challenging for the average worshipper to be sure they are keeping everyone happy!

Israel's neighbors typically understood that there was one lead or national deity, but there was not one all-powerful god among the many. When a country conquered another, it was standard practice to simply assimilate the conquered territory's deities into the home pantheon. And as each of the gods had a specialization that was either local or functional, there were great advantages to this practice. For example, in Canaan Ashtoreth was the goddess of Sidon, Milcom the god of Ammon, Chemosh the god of Moab, and Molech the god of Ammon (cf. 1 Kings 11:4–8). Each of these were bound to their own territory, so when Solomon allied with these countries, he also allied with their gods (not exactly God's plan). Perhaps the most well-known example of a functional specialization is Baal, the rain god and the god of fertility who was native to northern Canaan, and therefore a constant temptation to the Northern Kingdom. All said, when "each [sailor] cried out to his god" in Jonah 1:5, we are seeing polytheism in action. Each sailor was praying to the god of his own land begging for deliverance. And as these people did not share Jonah's ideas about monotheism, they had no problem with the whole host of heaven being petitioned at the same time!

Our People, Our Places, Our Faith

As we will discuss in the video lecture, one of the things that strikes me about the first chapter of the book of Jonah is that the heathens, the polytheists, the unbelievers were in many ways acting in a more ethical fashion than our prophet. They were doing everything in their power to keep him alive. But he had not offered them any sort of similar concern. He had put them at tremendous risk by attempting to hide from the God of heaven and earth in their ship's hold! Do we ever find ourselves as the community of faith in a similar spot? More concerned about our well-being than anyone else's? Can you think of an example? How do you think God feels about that?

The Sea

First Contact

Have you ever gotten thundered? That's what my kids and I call it when you're playing in the waves, everyone's laughing and splashing and diving, and out of the blue you get blindsided by a huge wave. You're knocked off your feet; sand is everywhere; you can't figure out which way is up. And even though you're only standing in three feet of water, in an instant you are reminded of the power of the sea and your own mortality! And everything in you starts shouting, "Get your head above water!"

Into the Book

In yesterday's reading we saw that Yahweh "hurled a great wind upon the sea, and there was a mighty temptest on the sea, so that the ship threatened to break up" and "the mariners were afraid" (1:4–5a ESV). In an attempt to find out who was guilty of bringing the storm upon them, the sailors "cast lots" and "the lot fell on Jonah" (1:7). This is where we pick up the story.

Jonah 1:8-10

⁸So they asked him, "Tell us, who is responsible for making all this trouble for us? What kind of work do you do? Where do you come from? What is your country? From what people are you?"

⁹He answered, "I am a Hebrew and I worship the LORD, the God of heaven, who made the sea and the dry land."

¹⁰This terrified them and they asked, "What have you done?" (They knew he was running away from the LORD, because he had already told them so.)

- Notice all of the questions the men ask Jonah in verse 8. Notice also in verse 9 that Jonah does not answer all of their questions. What *does* Jonah say about himself?

- Underline what Jonah says about Yahweh.

- Circle the effect Jonah's answer had on the men. Read the beginning of verse 10 in each of the following versions and circle the sailors' reaction to Jonah's answer.

NASB	NRSV	MSG	ESV
Then the men became extremely frightened and they said to him, "How could you do this?"	Then the men were even more afraid, and said to him, "What is this that you have done!"	At that, the men were frightened, really frightened, and said, "What on earth have you done!"	Then the men were exceedingly afraid and said to him, "What is this that you have done!"

- What was it in Jonah's answer that terrified them?

Real People, Real Places, Real Faith

For the people of the ancient Near East, the word "sea" is actually the name of a god. In the western Levant, that god was known as Yam; in the East as Tiamat. Tiamat was the personification of the primordial deep in the Babylonian creation epic. When she is defeated by the up-and-coming Marduk, and split in two "like a clam," the Mesopotamian equivalent of the heavens above and waters below are created under Marduk's kingship. Yam, on the other hand, was the Canaanite version of the sea god. Yam had an important temple in Ugarit (a major port city on the northern coast destroyed in 1200 BCE) and received regular offerings there. But Yam was ultimately defeated by the up-and-coming storm-god, Baal, who subsequently staked his claim in Canaan as the lead deity in what would become the territory of Israel. We know this story because Ugarit was not only an important center of trade, it contained within its ruins one of the most important Canaanite archives ever unearthed. By reading these ancient myths, we learn that the worldview in Jonah's time was that sea was not just a thing to the ancients, it was a person. And this person could be offended. Thus, when the sailors hear that the God that Jonah worships is the God of the earth and the *sea* they are terrified . . . or in the words of the ESV, "exceedingly afraid"!

Our People, Our Places, Our Faith

I find it interesting that the polytheists/pagans who are manning Jonah's ship are much more impressed with Yahweh's titles than the prophet is. Is this a matter of familiarity breeds contempt? Could this be an example of how we, the people of God, begin to take the fact that we worship the Lord of heaven and earth casually? An example of how *we*, the ones who should be his witnesses, begin to diminish him because we're too distracted (or perhaps too lazy) to pause over the fact that our God *hurls wind*? It is never good to take a superior for granted. It is particularly dangerous to take your God for granted. In the words of C. S. Lewis, he is "not like a *tame* lion."* Take a moment now and remind yourself that the God you claim cast the cosmos into place—and he is anything but tame.

---

*C. S. Lewis, *The Lion, the Witch, and the Wardrobe* in *The Complete Chronicles of Narnia* (New York: HarperCollins, 1998), 132.

To Appoint

A Word from the Author

With our second chapter, a second theme emerges in the book of Jonah. We go from "hurling" to "appointing" (Hebrew *mānāh*). And this time it is Yahweh who appoints. Yahweh had already appointed a missionary who refused to obey. He had already summoned a great wind to convince said prophet to obey. But it is clear at this point that Yahweh's free-will agent (that would be Jonah) is clearly not going to comply. So Yahweh pulls out the big guns—he now appoints a fish. A very big fish. A very big fish who will swallow our hero in order to help him along his way. In this chapter, we are reminded of a Creator who can find his servants anywhere they might wander (or hide), who is in no way bound by the earth he has created, who hurls wind, who appoints large aquatic mammals, and who can even fish out (sorry, pun intended) a man who is cascading into the mouth of Sheol itself. This is a God who cannot be resisted.

Real Time and Space

As far as we can tell, Jonah has succeeded in getting a significant distance away from Israel in the hold of his trade ship. As we will study in the video lecture, a number of trade ships from the Late Bronze Age (1550–1200 BCE) have been excavated from the depths of the Mediterranean, demonstrating that these ships did indeed sail the open sea. The size and draw of these ships made them extremely vulnerable (the Uluburun wreck was forty-nine feet long). But still the maritime economies of Phoenicia, Ugarit, and Egypt were very active and extremely lucrative! The trade route between the Nile Delta and the Phoenician capital city of Byblos has been documented back into the third millennium BCE, and there is a great deal of evidence that the island of Cyprus served as a hub for maritime activity throughout this ancient era. Not only did these ships transport timber, wine, and oil from the land of Israel, they also carried the exotic cargo conveyed to the port cities via the desert caravans—and all to the far reaches of the Mediterranean.

Hence, our hero finds himself out in the midst of the open sea, heading for the Spanish peninsula when the storm of storms hits. Hebrews were never known for any skill at seafaring. In fact, the only fleet of ships attributed to an Israelite king was Solomon's fleet docked at the southern port of Elath on the Red Sea (see 1 Kings 9:26). So we can be fairly sure that Jonah is way beyond his comfort zone, terrified by a storm of immense proportions, and convinced that this is his last gig.

DAY ONE

Jonah Overboard

First Contact

A big part of my childhood involved summers sailing on the Chesapeake Bay in a little twenty-six-foot sailboat. As my dad was a navy man, my four sisters and I were expected to serve as crew. And, therefore, we were also expected to know the difference between port and starboard, a sheet and a halyard, and how to reef a mainsail in a storm—this without any actual training. As a result of these adventures, I can say with some authority that there is nothing as exhilarating as running before a strong wind, under a cobalt blue sky at a hard heel, with the jib cinched down tight. I can also say with some authority that there is nothing more terrifying than that moment when the sky turns black, the wind does a 180, the sails go wild (with the halyards slapping against the mast like things possessed), and the boom comes flying across the cockpit without warning. In this moment any sane human is brought to the abrupt realization that they are merely mortal . . . and the sea is not.

Into the Book

When we last saw our sailors, they were terrified because they had just learned that Jonah was attempting to flee from Yahweh, not only the Creator

55

of the dry land but also the Creator of *the sea*! What are they going to do? Today's study will provide those answers.

Jonah 1:11-16

[11]The sea was getting rougher and rougher. So they asked him, "What should we do to you to make the sea calm down for us?"

[12]"Pick me up and throw me into the sea," he replied, "and it will become calm. I know that it is my fault that this great storm has come upon you."

[13]Instead, the men did their best to row back to land. But they could not, for the sea grew even wilder than before. [14]Then they cried out to the LORD, "Please, LORD, do not let us die for taking this man's life. Do not hold us accountable for killing an innocent man, for you, LORD, have done as you pleased." [15]Then they took Jonah and threw him overboard, and the raging sea grew calm. [16]At this the men greatly feared the LORD, and they offered a sacrifice to the LORD and made vows to him.

- What, if anything, surprises you about Jonah's answer to the sailors' question about what they needed to do?

- How did the men respond when Jonah told them the only way to calm the storm was to throw him into the sea?

- Who was it that prayed to Yahweh?

- What was their prayer?

- Underline the things the men did after hurling Jonah into the sea.

Real People, Real Places, Real Faith

As you read through this part of the narrative you can almost hear the panic in the voices of the men aboard the ship. You can envision these seasoned sailors struggling to row against the raging storm. You can hear the wind and the waves crashing against the boat and taste the salt water as it splashes in your face. And in the midst of all this chaos there is Jonah . . . "Yep, it's my fault. Pick me up and throw me in." He appears to show no emotion throughout this entire ordeal. Is he standing by watching as the sailors struggle with the oars? Is he begging for his life? Is he scrambling to throw *himself* in? What is he doing? The sailors are doing everything in their power to avoid hurling Jonah overboard, but they finally succumb to the inevitable and do just that. Did Jonah go willingly? Did he show any fear? The text doesn't say! A major reason for this is that the book is ancient, and it is representative of an equally ancient narrative genre that didn't waste space with emotion. So when you read that someone in this book is frightened, or angry, or compassionate . . . make sure you listen closely. Because if emotion is mentioned, it is a big deal. At this point in our story, we know the sailors are terrified. We also know that Jonah is in all likelihood facing his own death—he is a Hebrew (nonswimmer) in the middle of the Mediterranean far from land in the midst of a gigantic storm. Yet the fear we would anticipate remains unnamed. What we do get is "it's my fault you are in danger." So it is clear that Jonah has totally blown it and he knows it. But it is not at all clear that he has repented or is afraid. I'm intrigued by this. I'm more intrigued by the fact that as a result of Jonah's *disobedience*, the sailors aboard the ship have been introduced to the Creator of earth and sea.

Our People, Our Places, Our Faith

In the midst of trying to dodge God's will in his life, our hero winds up floating in the open ocean in the middle of a life-threatening storm. Not exactly Jonah's plan. But as you've seen above, the unbelievers who are watching this drama unfold are still finding in Jonah's life a witness to the character of his God. How interesting it is that even in those moments when we feel we have completely blown it (and sometimes we have), the fact that we have been with Jesus still shows.

Yahweh Appoints a Fish

First Contact

Warning: dad joke coming. Have you heard the one about the man stranded on his rooftop following a flood? He prayed that God would save him and believed that he would. So along came a man in a rowboat who told him to get in the boat. The man said, no, God would save him. Next there came a speedboat followed by a helicopter. Each time the man was invited to safety, each time his response was the same . . . he had faith in the Lord and the Lord would save him! When the flood continued to rise, the man eventually drowned. When he arrived before the Lord, the man asked why God hadn't saved him. The Lord responded: "I sent you two boats and a helicopter. What more did you expect?"

Into the Book

We ended yesterday's study with Jonah in the open sea, most likely expecting to drown. In today's reading we will see God send the most unexpected lifeguard of all time to rescue his wayward prophet. We will also look at passages from Genesis and Job that give us an idea of exactly how powerful Jonah's God is.

Genesis 1:20-21

²⁰And God said, "Let the waters bring forth swarms of living creatures, and let birds fly above the earth across the dome of the sky." ²¹So God created the great sea monsters and every living creature that moves, of every kind, with which the waters swarm, and every winged bird of every kind. And God saw that it was good. (NRSV)

■ What do you learn about God's relationship to his creation in this verse?

Jonah 1:17

¹⁷And the LORD appointed a great fish to swallow Jonah, and Jonah was in the stomach of the fish three days and three nights. (NASB)

■ Read this verse in the following translations. Underline the ways in which these versions translate the word "appointed."

KJV	MSG	NIV	NLT
Now the LORD had prepared a great fish to swallow up Jonah.	Then GOD assigned a huge fish to swallow Jonah.	Now the LORD provided a huge fish to swallow Jonah.	Now the LORD had arranged for a great fish to swallow Jonah.

■ What do you learn about God's relationship to his creation in this verse?

One sea creature notorious in the ancient world was also apparently somewhat mythological. Take a listen as God chastises Job for his hubris by speaking of this very scary inhabitant of the seas.

Job 41:1–34

[1]"Can you pull in Leviathan with a fishhook or tie down its tongue with a rope? [2]Can you put a cord through its nose or pierce its jaw with a hook? [3]Will it keep begging you for mercy? Will it speak to you with gentle words? [4]Will it make an agreement with you for you to take it as your slave for life? [5]Can you make a pet of it like a bird or put it on a leash for the young women in your house? [6]Will traders barter for it? Will they divide it up among the merchants? [7]Can you fill its hide with harpoons or its head with fishing spears? [8]If you lay a hand on it, you will remember the struggle and never do it again! [9]Any hope of subduing it is false; the mere sight of it is overpowering. [10]No one is fierce enough to rouse it. Who then is able to stand against me? [11]Who has a claim against me that I must pay? Everything under heaven belongs to me.

[12]"I will not fail to speak of Leviathan's limbs, its strength and its graceful form. [13]Who can strip off its outer coat? Who can penetrate its double coat of armor? [14]Who dares open the doors of its mouth, ringed about with fearsome teeth? [15]Its back has rows of shields tightly sealed together; [16]each is so close to the next that no air can pass between. [17]They are joined fast to one another; they cling together and cannot be parted. [18]Its snorting throws out flashes of light; its eyes are like the rays of dawn. [19]Flames stream from its mouth; sparks of fire shoot out. [20]Smoke pours from its nostrils as from a boiling pot over burning reeds. [21]Its breath sets coals ablaze, and flames dart from its mouth. [22]Strength resides in its neck; dismay goes before it. [23]The folds of its flesh are tightly joined; they are firm and immovable. [24]Its chest is hard as rock, hard as a lower millstone. [25]When it rises up, the mighty are terrified; they retreat before its thrashing. [26]The sword that reaches it has no effect, nor does the spear or the dart or the javelin. [27]Iron it treats like straw and bronze like rotten wood. [28]Arrows do not make it flee; slingstones are like chaff to it. [29]A club seems to it but a piece of straw; it laughs at the rattling of the lance. [30]Its undersides are jagged potsherds, leaving a trail in the mud like a threshing sledge. [31]It makes the depths churn like a boiling caldron and stirs up the sea like a pot of ointment. [32]It leaves a glistening

wake behind it; one would think the deep had white hair. [33]Nothing on earth is its equal—a creature without fear. [34]It looks down on all that are haughty; it is king over all that are proud."

- What do you learn about God and his relationship to his creation (specifically Leviathan) from these verses?

- As you read through the description of Leviathan, what creatures of your own experience (or the mythologies of our culture) come to mind? If you came face-to-face with this creature, what emotions do you think you would experience?

Real People, Real Places, Real Faith

As we heard in the opening lecture, many people view the book of Jonah as a children's story, an allegory, or a popular legend. Why? Because *there is a guy swallowed by a whale* in here! So one of the questions that the book of Jonah requires is the obvious one: "Is that possible?" In this session's lecture you will learn everything you ever wanted to know about large aquatic creatures that populate the Mediterranean Sea as we attempt to investigate this question via marine biology.

But we are also interested in the biblical character known as Leviathan. Leviathan is spoken of six times in the Old Testament: Job 3:8; 41:1–34; Amos 9:3; Psalm 74:13–23; Psalm 104:26; and Isaiah 27:1. Whereas in Job and the Psalms, Leviathan is understood as a beyond-belief creature that lives in the sea, and God is praised for having made something so amazing, in Isaiah 27:1, this same creature is transformed into a "tortuous (or twisted) serpent" who Yahweh must slay to bring peace to the planet. Most concur that this character (especially as described in Isaiah 27:1) emerges in part from the polytheistic mythology of Israel's neighbors. The creature is most clearly described in the Ugaritic Baal cycle. Here Baal (the lord of Canaan) is understood to have slain Leviathan, "the fleeing serpent . . . the tyrant with the seven heads"*; just as Yahweh will slay Leviathan at the end of all time in Isaiah 27:1. The language parallels between the two passages are too close to ignore. And when Psalm 74:13–14 is brought into play: "You divided the sea by your might; you broke the heads of the [dragons] sea monsters on the waters" (ESV), it is obvious that there is overlap here. Yahweh is apparently doing battle with an evil serpent known to Israel's broader world, just like Baal did.**

So what is this monster doing in the book of Jonah? And why is he now the submissive Labrador Retriever of the Most High? I would argue that once again our biblical authors are making an argument for Yahweh's supremacy over all the deities of their world. Just as Yahweh can command the sea to be quiet, he can whistle for Leviathan and Leviathan comes. Moreover, the Leviathan who is feared by all because of his violence, carefully swallows the prophet such that he does no harm. And rather than tearing Jonah to pieces as we would expect, gently delivers him to the shore so that the prophet can complete his calling. Essentially, what we hear from this passage from every angle is that Yahweh reigns supreme—over the sea, over Leviathan, and even over one very stubborn prophet.

Our People, Our Places, Our Faith

Like Jonah's story, our story doesn't happen in a vacuum. We are surrounded by circumstances and people and assumptions that are in constant conflict with our faith. As a result, attempting to be an obedient believer often leaves us swimming upstream. It also leaves us looking like the odd man out among our peers. The revelation of God's character we call "the Bible" speaks of this reality regularly. It is nothing new that God's people are living according to a different set of rules, answering to a different authority, building their lives on what appears to be an alien value system. And yet our God calls

---

*See tablet 5; CAT 1.5 I 1–3.
**See Wayne T. Pitard, "The Binding of Yamm: A New Edition of the Ugaritic Text KTU 1.83," *Journal of Near Eastern Studies* 57 (1998): 261–80.

us (and Jonah) to trust him in the midst of his redefinition of the world we *think* we see. Much like the famous movie *The Matrix*, what we think we see is not necessarily what really *is*. Is Leviathan a monster of mythic proportions that will swallow us up if we take a false step? Or is he the lap dog of the Almighty, awaiting his instructions just like the rest of us? As you close down this study today, remind yourself that you, too, are a creature, and that the Creator has all things in hand. You cannot make one hair on your head black or white (Matt. 5:36) and you don't have to. Let's not spend our best energy worrying about the things we cannot control. Let's take a lesson from Leviathan and simply come when we're called.

Yahweh Speaks to the Fish

First Contact

Have you ever gotten yourself into such a mess that you honestly couldn't tell which end was up? Where the circumstances had become so complicated that good or right or wise were all tangled up with really, really stupid? That season where you couldn't hear the voice of God for anything, and you were afraid to take any step any direction because you couldn't tell which path led toward better and which toward way worse? I'm going to guess that sitting in the first stomach of that large aquatic mammal, Jonah could relate.

Into the Book

Chapter 1 ends with Yahweh providing a great fish (Leviathan?) to retrieve Jonah from a stormy sea. As we will see, chapter 2 ends with Yahweh speaking to that great fish to deliver Jonah to the shore. Being the Creator of the universe and every living thing, it should be no surprise to us that God speaks to his creation and it responds.

Read the following verses from the book of Job. In these verses we read Yahweh's response to Job after Job had made his defense before his friends. Job has said (for thirty-seven chapters!) "I am not guilty!" and in his anger had begun to accuse God of injustice. In chapter 38, God shows up. Take a look at what he has to say. As you read, highlight all of the things in creation that God speaks to/commands in this beautiful oration. (For example, to what is God speaking in verse 11?)

Job 38:4-13, 34-35

4"Where were you when I laid the earth's foundation? Tell me, if you understand. 5Who marked off its dimensions? Surely you know! Who stretched a measuring line across it? 6On what were its footings set, or who laid its cornerstone—7while the morning stars sang together and all the angels shouted for joy?

8"Who shut up the sea behind doors when it burst forth from the womb, 9when I made the clouds its garment and wrapped it in thick darkness, 10when I fixed limits for it and set its doors and bars in place, 11when I said, 'This far you may come and no farther; here is where your proud waves halt'?

12"Have you ever given orders to the morning, or shown the dawn its place, 13that it might take the earth by the edges and shake the wicked out of it? . . .

34"Can you raise your voice to the clouds and cover yourself with a flood of water? 35Do you send the lightning bolts on their way? Do they report to you, 'Here we are'?"

Job 39:26-27

26"Is it by your understanding that the hawk soars and spreads his wings toward the south? 27Is it at your command that the eagle mounts up and makes his nest on high?" (ESV)

■ How much do you know about Job? Without any research, list three of those things here.

- In light of the fact that you probably wrote "a person who suffered terribly" in your list, what is *your* first response to Yahweh's response to him?

- As you ponder this passage, what do you think about Job's God?

- In light of how and what God says, what do you think God wanted Job to think?

Jonah 2:10

[10]And the Lord spoke to the fish, and it vomited Jonah out upon the dry land. (ESV)

- Compare Jonah 2:10 to Jonah 1:4 (Week Three, Day Two) and notice the actions of Yahweh. How would you describe Yahweh based on these two verses? Give me at least three modifiers.

Real People, Real Places, Real Faith

One of my past students, Eden Parker, penned these words:

In the book of Jonah, we hear about the Lord "appointing" a fish, a plant, a worm, and the wind for tasks. None of them complain or rebel. But when the Lord appoints his prophet, who knows him in a way none of these can, the prophet turns and runs. No, these characters in creation cannot speak, but in this story, through the literary art of the Hebrew language, God has let them speak. They tell of the tragedy of our disobedience. They tell of the great beauty in obedience. They remind us what we lost when we ate the fruit, when we decided to believe the lies that God's Word isn't true and his way is not best.

Yes, I am a fish. But fish have stories too.
Anyway, it was a regular day and I was doing what fish do.
It was not a fancy day so I expected nothing new.
And in a moment—in a flash—I heard *His* very voice.
Him! Yes, He, the Maker, who lets me wander His very own sea.
"Up!" He said, "I have appointed you with a special task today."
And then He asked me to serve Him in this way:
One of those special creatures—a real live child of God—
I was asked to carry across the sea.
Oh to be like them: made to know God like a friend
And be made like Him, specially.
So, I went.
And I picked him up in the strangest fashion.
He was nearly drowning and had not a single possession.
"Swallow him? Really?" I asked the Maker.
"Alright, if that is what you say. I won't see it as silly."
Then after I swallowed him,
Obeying even when it felt funny,
The strangest thing I heard from my tummy.
The man was crying and even starting to sing!
With great pain he did this and I wondered to myself,
How had he gotten so beside himself?
Three days the Maker told me to keep him on board,
Until I should spit him onto Nineveh's shore.

Now that I look back,
I don't know why God chose me for that task.
I don't know what the Maker was doing with this man,
But, I rejoice that I got to be part of His plan.
I don't know what in the world this was for,
But I am thankful I got to serve my Lord.
So . . . if you're a son or daughter of the Maker—
One of those special image bearers—

But you're thinking of getting on an escape boat,
Please don't get on board.
Instead, think of my story
And happily serve the Lord.

—Eden Parker, 2015

Our People, Our Places, Our Faith

Last week we challenged you to remember that your God is not a tame lion. In that lesson we were challenged by this in the context of his sovereign power over an immense and immensely complex universe. Let me challenge you again with this truth that C. S. Lewis has taught us all. He is not a tame lion. Sometimes what God does doesn't make sense to us. Sometimes, the back side of the tapestry doesn't portray the picture being embroidered on the front side clearly. Sometimes we are being utilized as part of a plan we cannot see. Sometimes the deliverance from our debacle looks way scarier than the debacle itself. And sometimes God is calling us to simply trust him in the in-between space. Name your in-between space today. Ask him to step into it with you. And ask him to give you the strength you need to trust him to follow through.

WEEK SIX

A Second Chance

A Word from the Author

In this past video lesson we explored the $64,000 question—is there a large aquatic creature that frequents the Mediterranean who has the capacity to swallow an adult male human without dismembering him? Then we asked if that same creature could also regurgitate that human. And *if* regurgitated, we asked if it would be possible for that human to survive the process. After exploring the cast of characters available (the sperm whale and great white shark, in particular) and several testimonies from the whaling industry of the eighteenth and nineteenth centuries, we determined that it is quite possible for a sperm whale—with their gulping feeding habit and penchant for giant squid—to swallow a human whole. We also learned that sperm whales have more than one stomach and are notorious for vomiting up weird stuff. But could a human survive such an event? As we determined in our last session . . . that would probably take a miracle. But of course, that would be the point.

So we are still in chapter 2. Still in the chapter introducing our second literary theme, the word *mānāh* ("to appoint"). Although God *had* appointed his prophet to travel to Nineveh and preach the good news of Yahweh's forgiveness, he has had to resort to appointing a whale to come retrieve said prophet in his rebellion. As I said in lecture, I picture a Border Collie (or perhaps an Australian Shepherd?) responding to his master's whistle, trotting over to retrieve the holy man, and carefully placing him on the dry ground where he should have been headed in the first place.

So as chapter 2 opens, let me emphasize again that getting swallowed by this whale is not some sort of further punishment directed at Jonah for disobedience. The great fish is not the villain here. Rather, the great fish is Jonah's deliverance. This is clear from the fact that Jonah responds to being swallowed with a hymn of praise! Jonah's testimony of that deliverance is going to be a major focus of this week's study.

Real Time and Space

As you read this psalm, ask yourself how Jonah is feeling about this fish right now. Although we've been taught to see the whale as Jonah's antagonist, remember how we got to this point in the narrative. Remember that Jonah is trying to flee Yahweh's territorial boundaries by getting on a ship headed for Tarshish. Remember that unlike the other ancient Near Eastern gods, Yahweh doesn't *have* territorial boundaries, so Yahweh, the God of earth and sea, *hurls* a great wind at Jonah's ship to stop him, resulting in the sailors *hurling* Jonah into the sea to save the ship. In light of the fact that our prophet is currently dog-paddling in the middle of the Mediterranean, I think it is fair to say that Jonah is feeling pretty good about this whale about now. Yahweh is indeed the God of land and sea, and as this psalm makes very clear, Yahweh can find and mind his servant whatever the crisis at hand.

As we work through this week's lesson, keep in mind that it would be quite a stretch to anticipate that Jonah had a pen and paper on hand in the midst of his near-drowning and rescue. Moreover, the chances that the prophet remained conscious and composed enough throughout to write a psalm is even more challenging. But like any faithful Israelite, we can anticipate that Jonah had memorized many psalms, creeds, and hymns, and probably called several to mind between the hurling, drowning, and swallowing. Jonah 2:2–9 is the end result of those cries for help and expressions of gratitude. Particularly interesting in Jonah's prayer are the parallels with Psalm 18—which might indeed have been the memorized piece that Jonah recited as he stared his own mortality in the face.

Jonah's Song of Deliverance and Psalm of Praise

First Contact

What is a verse or song that gets you through difficult times? During World War II Corrie ten Boom and her sister Betsie were prisoners at Ravensbruck, a women's Nazi death camp. Miraculously, Corrie and Betsie managed to smuggle a Bible into the camp. On the edge of starvation, huddled into over-crowded, filthy, flea- and lice-infested dormitories, these women survived by clinging to the Scripture they read daily. At one point of particular desperation Corrie said, "How can we live in such a place?!" Recalling what they had read in their Bible that day, Betsie replied that God had already given them the answer: "'Give thanks in all circumstances!' That's what we can do!"* Betsie followed up with a prayer thanking God . . . for the fleas!

---

*Corrie ten Boom, with Elizabeth and John Sherrill, *The Hiding Place* 35th Anniversary Edition (Grand Rapids, MI: Chosen, 2006), 209.

Into the Book

The last time we saw Jonah he was in the middle of the sea. But our narrator has not, up until this point, provided us with any clues as to Jonah's emotional state. But in his prayer in chapter 2, for the first time in this book we are given insight into what is going on in his heart. The great man of God, who has intentionally, willfully defied the command of his God, who has been given a second chance, offers us a prayer of thanksgiving . . . from the belly of a whale. As we have already discussed, this prayer on Jonah's part probably arose from other memorized hymns and liturgies from his past. One such parallel is Jonah's prayer found in 2:2–9 and David's song of deliverance found in Psalm 18. As you read through these passages, look for those similarities.

Jonah 2:2–9	Psalm 18:1–6
²"From my distress, I called out to Yahweh, and he answered me; out of the belly of Sheol I cried, and you heard my voice. ³For you cast me into the deep, into the heart of the seas, and the flood surrounded me; all your waves and your billows passed over me. ⁴Then I said, 'I am driven away from your sight; yet I shall again look upon your holy temple.' ⁵The waters closed in over me to take my life; the deep surrounded me; weeds were wrapped about my head ⁶at the roots of the mountains. I went down to the land whose bars closed upon me forever; yet you brought up my life from the pit, O Yahweh my God. ⁷When my life was fainting away, I remembered the LORD, and my prayer came to you, into your holy temple. ⁸Those who pay regard to vain idols forsake their hope of steadfast love. ⁹But I with the voice of thanksgiving will sacrifice to you; what I have vowed I will pay. Salvation belongs to Yahweh!" (author's paraphrase)	¹I love you, O Yahweh, my strength. ²Yahweh is my rock and my fortress and my deliverer, my God, my rock, in whom I take refuge, my shield, and the horn of my salvation, my stronghold. ³I call upon the LORD, who is worthy to be praised, and I am saved from my enemies. ⁴The cords of death encompassed me; the torrents of destruction assailed me; ⁵the cords of Sheol entangled me; the snares of death confronted me. ⁶In my distress I called upon Yahweh; to my God I cried for help. From his temple he heard my voice, and my cry to him reached his ears. (author's paraphrase)

- In Jonah 2:3–6a, highlight all of the things that Jonah describes happening to him (for example, "the flood surrounded me").

- In verse 6b, what does Jonah credit Yahweh with doing? What do you think "the pit" is?

- When was it that Jonah cried out to Yahweh (v. 7)?

- What was Jonah sure was going to happen to him?

- Using a colored pencil, underline all of Jonah's quotations or near-quotations of Psalm 18:1–6.

- Now, go back to verse 2. What do you think Jonah refers to when he says "out of the belly of Sheol"? Do you think he is speaking of the belly of the fish or something else?

- Why do you think both David and Jonah speak of the temple?

- What did Jonah promise Yahweh for his deliverance?

Real People, Real Places, Real Faith

Jonah cried "out of the belly of Sheol." What is "Sheol"? In general, Sheol is understood as the place of the dead, the grave, or the underworld. In the Old Testament, Sheol (also referred to as the "pit") is simply death and the grave. Whereas, in the New Testament, Sheol—often translated simply as "death"—seems to also be taking on the connotation of hell (cf. Acts 2:27; Revelation 1:18; 20:13). Indeed, even in the Old Testament, death is generally thought of as a place of darkness, dust, and silence (Job 17:13, 16; Ecclesiastes 9:5; Psalms 88:12; 94:17*), but it is not associated with divine* *punishment or pain*. For the Israelites, it is a place where one continued to exist as a shade or spirit in a form different from life on earth. Whether or not that existence had any contact with the divine presence of Yahweh, or if there was a second stage to death as there is in the New Testament (first physical death, and then a post-judgment place of either reward or punishment) is unclear from the Old Testament Scriptures. Of great interest to us here, though, is that the sea was broadly recognized as an *entrance into Sheol*. And thus, its deep, dark, unexplored depths were terrifying. If you went in . . . you would never come out.

Our People, Our Places, Our Faith

According to newer studies in neuroscience, neuroplasticity in particular, it is possible to *teach* and *reteach* your brain to respond to stimulus in a particular fashion. As a result, a person can actually train their brain to respond to the stimulus of stress with calm as opposed to anxiety; the stimulus of a particular substance or habit with abstinence; the stimulus of crisis with optimism. This new insight is why books like *The Stress-Proof Brain* and *Why Zebras Don't Get Ulcers* are flying off the shelves. It would seem to me that this is not actually new information (although, of course, now it can be scientifically quantified). For centuries the Scriptures have been commanding us to do the same—change the way you respond to crisis! So for example, Philippians 4:4–6: "Rejoice in the Lord always; again I will say, rejoice. Let your reasonableness be known to everyone. The Lord is at hand; *do not be anxious about anything*, but in everything by prayer and supplication with thanksgiving let your requests be made known to God" (ESV, emphasis added). A command to respond to stress with prayer is a command to rewire your brain; it is a command to retrain our brains to respond to a particular stimulus with a different response. In his despair, Jonah cried out to God. He chose to pray in the midst of some really serious stress. He found hope in the midst of despair. Paul commands the same—change your response to stimulus! Are you anxious? Pretty sure this is the final curtain call? Try praying. Not just about the standard prayer list stuff, but about what you *really* are stressed about. And let's get neuroplasticity working in our favor!

Jonah's Psalm Compared to Psalms

First Contact

Do you know the game Would You Rather? Give it a go. Would you rather have someone you work with barge into your office to duke out a conflict, or have that same person simply exclude you from every department e-mail or report they send? Would you rather have your spouse blow up at you about something they think you did, or give you the cold shoulder and silent treatment for a month? Would you rather have your best friend text you that they don't want to be friends anymore, or have them simply (and silently) stop interacting with you?

Into the Book

Today we're going to continue looking at Jonah's psalm, in particular for echoes from other psalms.

Pull out your colored pencils or highlighters and for each of the following passages, highlight all of Jonah's quotations or near-quotations of the psalms using different colors to see the parallels.

Ref	Jonah (ESV)	Ref	Psalms (ESV)
2:2a	"I called out to the LORD, out of my distress, and he answered me;	120:1	In my distress I called to the LORD, and he answered me.
2:2b	"out of the belly of Sheol I cried, and you heard my voice.	30:3	O LORD, you have brought up my soul from Sheol; you restored me to life from among those who go down to the pit.
2:3a	"For you cast me into the deep, into the heart of the seas, and the flood surrounded me;	88:6–7	You have put me in the depths of the pit, in the regions dark and deep. [7] Your wrath lies heavy upon me, and you overwhelm me with all your waves.
2:3b	"all your waves and your billows passed over me	42:7	Deep calls to deep at the roar of your waterfalls; all your breakers and your waves have gone over me.
2:4a	"Then I said, 'I am driven away from your sight;'	31:22a	I had said in my alarm, "I am cut off from your sight."
2:4b	"'yet I shall again look upon your holy temple.'"	5:7	But I, through the abundance of your steadfast love, will enter your house. I will bow down toward your holy temple in the fear of you.

2:5a	"The waters closed in over me to take my life;"	69:1–2	Save me, O God! For the waters have come up to my neck. ² I sink in deep mire, where there is no foothold; I have come into deep waters, and the flood sweeps over me.
2:6b	"yet you brought up my life from the pit, O LORD my God."	103:4	who redeems your life from the pit, who crowns you with steadfast love and mercy,
2:7a	"When my life was fainting away, I remembered the LORD,"	142:3	When my spirit faints within me, you know my way! In the path where I walk they have hidden a trap for me.
2:8a	"Those who pay regard to vain idols forsake their hope of steadfast love."	31:6	I hate those who pay regard to worthless idols, but I trust in the LORD.
2:9a	"But I with the voice of thanksgiving will sacrifice to you; what I have vowed I will pay."	50:14	Offer to God a sacrifice of thanksgiving, and perform your vows to the Most High
2:9c	"Salvation belongs to the LORD!"	3:8	Salvation belongs to the LORD; your blessing be on your people!

Real People, Real Places, Real Faith

One of the most amazing things about Israel's God is that he actually *speaks* to his people. As we reviewed in our study on the office of the prophet, whereas other deities claimed to communicate to their people via the entrails of ritually sacrificed animals, Yahweh actually *speaks* to his people through his prophet. How ironic it is that *our* prophet launches his psalm with his affirmation that God has spoken to *him*. "I called out to Yahweh and he *answered* me!" He answered me! In the polytheistic world of Israel's neighbors, this was not normative. Do you remember the captain of the trade ship? "Get up! Call on your god! Perhaps your god will be concerned about us and we will not perish!" Do you remember how amazed the sailors were when Jonah's God actually *did* something about the storm? The prophets of Israel were constantly reminding the people of Israel that their idols (statues of false gods) had eyes that couldn't actually see, and ears that couldn't actually hear. But Yahweh does see and does hear, and does respond. This is why the "vain idols" are mocked in the previous passages. These psalms of thanksgiving are contrasting the blind, deaf, unmoving statues of their neighbors with the invisible and omnipotent Yahweh. In Isaiah 44:12–17, Isaiah took the message further and ridiculed those who carve their own god out of a block of wood and then think that god can answer in a time of crisis! In our crisis in chapter 2 of the book of Jonah, we see an entirely different picture. The prophet knew he was facing certain death, so he prayed . . . and Yahweh (who can see and hear and act) saw his calamity, heard his cry, and *answered him*.

Our People, Our Places, Our Faith

Our first contact for this day's study was a little exercise. It was designed to pull out those incredibly frustrating emotions that come from a relationship where open communication has broken down. When the only choices left are yelling and passive-aggressive silent treatment. Which did you choose? I know for me, if I truly care about the relationship, I'll take yelling over silence any day. Silence means that my colleague, friend, spouse is more interested in protecting themselves than they are in their relationship with me. And in my life experience, that is the death knell of relationship. Now don't get me wrong, I don't want to be yelled at any more than the next person, but I would rather deal with a living, irritated relationship, than a dying, retreating one. Which would you rather? A god who gave you the silent treatment, or one that might need to yell at you a bit? I think I'll take the latter.

Jonah's Second Chance

First Contact

Have you ever been in a place where you really wanted a do-over? Maybe you're a golfer and on the first tee your shot goes wrong and you say, "I'll take my mulligan" (a.k.a. "do-over"). Or maybe your child is playing a game that isn't going his way and you hear him from the other room saying, "I want a do-over!" Or maybe it was something more serious. Maybe it was something you said to a friend that you immediately regretted and you wish you could take it back and have a second try. Or something even more grave—when you said yes, even though your vows clearly stated that your answer should have been no. In a circumstance where you've blown it, you knew it, and all you really wanted was a second chance, did you get one?

Into the Book

Yahweh delivered Jonah from certain death by means of the great fish, and then Yahweh told the fish to vomit Jonah onto dry ground. What lots of readers have missed over the years is that Yahweh was giving Jonah a second chance, a do-over.

Jonah 3:1-3

¹Then the word of the Lord came to Jonah a second time: ²"Go to the great city of Nineveh and proclaim to it the message I give you."

³Jonah obeyed the word of the Lord and went to Nineveh. Now Nineveh was a very large city; it took three days to go through it.

- Let's remind ourselves *why* Jonah didn't go the first time. List three reasons here.

- Do you see anything in this passage that speaks to Jonah repenting or God forgiving?

- How does the narrator handle Jonah's second chance here?

- What are the results of Jonah seizing his second chance and following through on God's original command?

- Compare what has happened here to Jonah with what happens to Ananias in the New Testament.

Acts 9:10-20

¹⁰Now there was a disciple at Damascus named Ananias; and the Lord said to him in a vision, "Ananias." And he said, "Here I am, Lord." ¹¹And the Lord said to him, "Get up and go to the street called Straight, and inquire at the house of Judas for a man from Tarsus named Saul, for he is praying, ¹²and he has seen in a vision a man named Ananias come in and lay his hands on him, so that he might regain his sight." ¹³But Ananias answered, "Lord, I have heard from many about this man, how much harm he did to Your saints at Jerusalem; ¹⁴and here he has authority from the chief priests to bind all who call on Your name." ¹⁵But the Lord said to him, "Go, for he is a chosen

instrument of Mine, to bear My name before the Gentiles and kings and the sons of Israel; ¹⁶for I will show him how much he must suffer for My name's sake." ¹⁷So Ananias departed and entered the house, and after laying his hands on him said, "Brother Saul, the Lord Jesus, who appeared to you on the road by which you were coming, has sent me so that you may regain your sight and be filled with the Holy Spirit." ¹⁸And immediately there fell from his eyes something like scales, and he regained his sight, and he got up and was baptized . . . ²⁰and immediately he began to proclaim Jesus in the synagogues, saying, "He is the Son of God." (NASB)

- Who told Ananias to go to the street called Straight and visit Saul?

- Why didn't Ananias want to go to Saul the first time he was called? List three reasons here.

- Did Ananias go anyway? Why?

- Do you see anything in this passage that communicates that Ananias repented or God forgave?

- How does the narrator handle Ananias's second chance?

- What are the results of Ananias seizing his second chance and following through on God's original command?

Real People, Real Places, Real Faith

We discussed the Assyrians in a previous video lesson—an empire notorious for its unending military activity and brutality toward the conquered. Because we are dealing with real people, who lived in real places, we are dealing with a real prophet who was full of both fear and disdain. As a result, Jonah said no. Jonah said no largely because the Assyrians were dangerous. And in our study today we've seen that Ananias said no for the same reason—Saul was dangerous. These are rational responses. But in both cases God had something bigger in mind. In both cases the front of the tapestry looked very different from the back. I am reminded of the story of David Wilkerson, the coauthor of *The Cross and the Switchblade* (1962). This is the man who founded Teen Challenge. A child of a preacher himself, he served as a minister in the Assemblies of God in small (safe) churches in rural Pennsylvania throughout the 1950s. In 1958, he saw a photograph in *Life* magazine of seven teenagers who had been arrested for gang violence in New York City, and he felt compelled by the Holy Spirit to "go to Nineveh" (that would be the drug-infested bowels of NYC). So he went. And began a street ministry to young drug addicts and gang members, which eventually evolved into the residential recovery program now known as Teen Challenge—a program where thousands of young adults have found safe space, freedom from addiction, and a new lease on life. Wilkerson also founded and pastored Times Square Church, a large community of faith that continues to thrive in NYC. At the time, Times Square was known as a center of X-rated films, strip clubs, live peep shows, prostitution, and drug addiction. Wilkerson states that walking down 42nd Street one night, "I saw 9-, 10- and 11-year-old kids bombed on crack cocaine . . . I wept and prayed, 'God, you've got to raise up a testimony in this hellish place.'" God's answer was, "You do it."* And so he did. So we ask ourselves, were the heroin addicts, pimps, dealers, and gang members of NYC dangerous? Heck yes. Did Wilkerson answer the call anyway? Yes again. Did it make a difference? Check out Teen Challenge on Google sometime and answer that one for yourself.

Our People, Our Places, Our Faith

What we learn from each of these stories is that sometimes God's call doesn't appear to make sense. Sometimes, the plan seems either way too hard or

---

*"The History of Times Square Church: A Testimony of Obedience" tsc.nyc/history/ retrieved October 17, 2018.

way too dangerous. Now don't get me wrong, we need to be very careful about doing something super edgy because we *think* the Holy Spirit has spoken to us. But in each of these cases, God *had* spoken. And each of these men was expected to respond. The first two started with no; and they both needed a do-over. And God gave them one. A lot like he gave the Ninevites a do-over. Do you need a do-over today? Did you say no when you should have said yes? Or did you say yes when you should have said no? Either way, my friend, this God we are talking about is indeed a God of second chances. So get up. Try again. Failure is only the first chapter . . . not the last.

A Compassionate God and a (Very) Angry Prophet

A Word from the Author

As we step into chapter 3, we step into a third literary theme as well, "to announce" (Hebrew *qārā'*). So we have now gone from "hurling" (Hebrew *ṭûl*) in chapter 1, to "appointing" (Hebrew *mānāh*) in chapter 2, to "announcing" (*qārā'*) in chapter 3. Last week we saw that Jonah, the great man of God, the messenger of the Almighty, who had intentionally and willfully defied the command of his God . . . was given a second chance. As we've seen, Jonah had responded to his calling with cognitive dissonance—the mental discomfort experienced by a person who simultaneously holds two or more contradictory beliefs. As a prophet, it was his task to announce the word of God. But as an Israelite, a member of the theocracy of Israel whose standard audience was *Israel*, how could Jonah bring a word of forgiveness to *Assyrians*? Hence, his cognitive dissonance.

Theocracy: a human government that is ruled by God.

This is one of the reasons that Jonah did not want to go to Nineveh—because he thought the gifts of God were only for the people of God. Under the Mosaic covenant this was an understandable mistake. Yet in this strategic story (the *only* story we have from the prophet Jonah) we all learn that the nationalism born of theocracy in the Mosaic covenant is not all there is to God's larger plan. And we learn right along with Jonah that God's vision for the world is not actually new with the new covenant. Alas, Jonah had not quite adjusted to that idea yet.

Real Time and Space

As we have discussed in lecture, Assyria was an ancient empire. It was first established as the Dynasty of Agade under Sargon I in 2300 BCE. (His name means "legitimate king"—you can *hear* the political intrigue behind that one!) Under his rule, for the first time, all of Mesopotamia was united under a single monarch, and this would become the paradigm for following rulers of every nation. This Old Assyrian Empire and the following Middle Assyrian Empire (established 1350 BCE) were known for military crusades, broad trade initiatives, and their ultimate ambition to control all the land between the two rivers. And although many of these kings were extremely successful in these endeavors, the millennium and a half following Sargon I will see extreme fluctuations in the political fortunes of the region. The rulers of the southern nations (Sumer, Babylonia, and Elam), Mittani and the Hittites to the north and west, and the Amorites of Mari in the middle-Euphrates region will all push back against the ambitions of the Assyrian monarchs and the 1,500 years of history between Sargon I and the rise of the Neo-Assyrian Empire will be just as complex and conflicted as 1,500 years of history in Europe, the far East, or Africa.

Perhaps most important to our reading of the book of Jonah is to realize that during these centuries the religions of Mesopotamia become equally complex. There were *hundreds* of gods honored in the region. Each ethnic group and city had its own deities, and as was typical to polytheism, there was a broad tolerance for the existence, celebration, and fluid identity of these many gods and goddesses. So, for example, the Sumerian high god

Anu of the city of Uruk was understood as the father of Enlil, who decreed the fates and brought kingship to humanity and might be found at the city of Nippur. Aššur, the head of the Old Assyrian pantheon (who, of course, could be found in the city of Aššur) would eventually be syncretized with Enlil by the Assyrians, as would Marduk by the Babylonians.

Our city, Nineveh (settled as early as 6000 BCE), served as the religious center for worship of the goddess Inanna/Ištar (the goddess of love and war) . . . who also happened to be the twin sister of Šamaš, the god of the sun and of justice (located at Sippar and Larsa). These, and a dozen other major gods and goddesses were accompanied by a multitude of demons, spirits, and the ghosts of unhappy ancestors in the spiritual realm of Mesopotamia. Thus, the kings of Assyria and Babylonia, Mari and Elam all understood themselves as agents of the gods, responsible to build their temples, fight their wars, and carry out their wishes.

All said, it is important for us as students of the Bible to keep in mind that *our* heroes don't even step onto the stage of world history until the settlement in Canaan in 1200 BCE. They don't step onto the international political stage until the monarchy (1000 BCE). And we can be sure that their strange concept of *monotheism* and the backwoods, regional deity they are worshipping—Yahweh—would not garner any interest from the ancient religious systems of Mesopotamia. If our book of Jonah is indeed contemporary with the Jonah of 2 Kings 14:23–29, then we are looking at 800–745 BCE as our arena of real time. This era, as detailed in lecture, was part of a larger era of stagnation and decline in Assyria. This recession not only depleted the luxurious lifestyle of the royal courts, destabilized economies, and sent regular paycheck-to-paycheck citizens scrambling to make ends meet, it convinced the locals that there must be some god somewhere who was unhappy with them.

For Assyria, the official borders of the nation didn't change, but the provincial governors begin to behave as independent rulers, and surrounding people groups (the tribes of Urartu in particular) started encroaching. Perhaps of greatest interest to those tracking the impact of Jonah's preaching is that on June 15, 763 BCE—in addition to the existing array of economic and military problems in Assyria—the sun disappeared from 9:33 a.m. to 12:19 p.m.!* A total eclipse of the sun is always a big deal. But when you happen to be a polytheist, and one of your primary deities is Šamaš (the god of the sun who is also the twin brother of your patron deity), and he hides his face for three full hours . . . well, I can guarantee you that everyone in Nineveh was more than a little nervous. The question on every heart from the governor's seat to the fisherman's hut was the same: Which deity is angry with us and why?

---

*Michael Roaf, *Cultural Atlas of Mesopotamia and the Ancient Near East* (Oxford Press, 1990), 175.

A Compassionate God

First Contact

On a recent playdate with his best little girl friend, Penny, Kathy's almost four-year-old son did something he *knew* that he was not supposed to do . . . he hit his friend. From the next room Mama heard Penny's little voice calling for reinforcements. Before she even reached the playroom, Kathy could hear Joshua pleading for a reprieve, "I'm sorry, Penny! I'm sorry! No Penny, please don't tell my mommy, I'm sorry!" If you've ever been privy to one of these crises, you will not be surprised that Penny was not actually particularly hurt (no tears). But she was very invested in making sure Joshua was punished for his crime. Tears streaming down his face, Joshua begged for absolution. But in the world of four-year-olds, this might be the big one and Penny knew it. After some handy mediation on Kathy's part, Joshua's apology was accepted, hugs were exchanged, and Penny and Joshua went back to their Little People village with nary a thought as to the relational precipice they had just navigated. Ah, if only adult life were so simple.

Into the Book

After being regurgitated on the shore and told again to go to Nineveh, this time Jonah went and the only recorded words we have of his message are

"Forty days more, and Nineveh shall be overthrown!" (3:4 NRSV). We also have the response of the Ninevites to this message.

Jonah 3:5-10

⁵The Ninevites believed God. A fast was proclaimed, and all of them, from the greatest to the least, put on sackcloth.

⁶When Jonah's warning reached the king of Nineveh, he rose from his throne, took off his royal robes, covered himself with sackcloth and sat down in the dust. ⁷This is the proclamation he issued in Nineveh:

"By the decree of the king and his nobles:

Do not let people or animals, herds or flocks, taste anything; do not let them eat or drink. ⁸But let people and animals be covered with sackcloth. Let everyone call urgently on God. Let them give up their evil ways and their violence. ⁹Who knows? God may yet relent and with compassion turn from his fierce anger so that we will not perish."

¹⁰When God saw what they did and how they turned from their evil ways, he relented and did not bring on them the destruction he had threatened.

- Highlight the things the *people* did in verse 5.

- Highlight the things the *king* did in verses 6–7.

- Underline the king's instructions. To whom did the king's proclamation extend?

- What was the reason the king instructed the inhabitants to do these things?

- What is the significance of the sackcloth?

- Compare 1:6 with 3:9. What similarities do you notice?

1:6The captain went to [Jonah] and said, "How can you sleep? Get up and call on your god! Maybe he will take notice of us so that we will not perish."	3:9"Who knows? God may yet relent and with compassion turn from his fierce anger so that we will not perish."

■ Now compare 1:15–16 with 3:10. What similarities do you notice?

1:15Then [the sailors] took Jonah and threw him overboard, and the raging sea grew calm. 16At this the men greatly feared the LORD, and they offered a sacrifice to the LORD and made vows to him.	3:10When God saw what they did, how they turned from their evil ways, he relented [changed his mind] and did not bring on them the destruction he had threatened.

■ What is God's response to the humility and repentance of the sailors and the Ninevites?

■ What do these passages teach you about the character of Jonah's God?

■ What aspects of that character seem to still be missing in the character of our prophet?

Real People, Real Places, Real Faith

Putting on sackcloth, fasting, sitting on the ground or low to the ground, and covering one's head with ash were all well-known in Israel's world as signs of mourning, despair, and repentance. Sackcloth is a material much like burlap, made out of camel or goat hair. The sackcloth would be worn directly on the skin, and choosing to wear this *very* uncomfortable clothing demonstrated grief and self-affliction.

One of the earliest examples in our Bible is found in Genesis 37:34. Here Jacob's sons had come to their father with Joseph's robe covered in blood.

When Jacob saw it, he "tore his clothes, put on sackcloth and mourned for his son many days." Following the death of Abner, his commander, King David commanded all the people to "tear your clothes and put on sackcloth and walk in mourning in front of Abner" (2 Sam. 3:31). Hezekiah did the same when Jerusalem was surrounded and besieged by the Assyrian army. After hearing the words of the commander of the Assyrian army, Hezekiah, in desperation, "tore his clothes and put on sackcloth and went into the temple of the LORD" (2 Kings 19:1). Several hundred years later, the book of Esther offers another dramatic example. Here the king of Persia had just signed a decree to annihilate all of the Jews throughout the province. When Mordecai, Esther's cousin, heard this news "he tore his clothes, put on sackcloth and ashes . . . In every province to which the edict and order of the king came, there was great mourning among the Jews, with fasting, weeping and wailing. Many lay in sackcloth and ashes" (Esther 4:1, 3).

To this day, when a Jewish family loses a loved one they "sit shiva"—meaning they mourn for a full week. Customs include sitting low to the ground, covering the mirrors in their homes, and tearing their garments. On the highest holy day of the Jewish calendar, the Day of Atonement, Jews seek forgiveness for wrongs done against God and against other human beings. The evening and day of Yom Kippur are marked by twenty-five hours of fasting and around-the-clock public and private prayer. All of these customs echo back to what we see in the Old Testament. To mourn the loss of a loved one or to express grief for one's own sin is to adopt the posture, clothing, and actions that communicate the realities of loss and failure.

In the case of the Ninevites, after hearing the Lord's message they "believed God" (3:5). Now exactly what the extent of their knowledge of who this God was or what he was like is a matter of debate. But the response is that the king (a servant of the gods) immediately launched a citywide fast complete with sackcloth and ashes. Their mourning is a recognition that they have offended. And their hope is that by their fasting and postures of repentance: "Who knows? God may relent and change his mind; he may turn from his fierce anger, so that we do not perish."

Our People, Our Places, Our Faith

When I get to this place in Jonah's story, I cannot help but notice that both the sailors and the king—pagans to the core—recognize that they need to repent. But they don't know to whom they should be repenting. They have a generic concept that a deity is angry . . . but which one and why? How is it we have a *prophet* on hand in both the crisis of the storm and the crisis in Nineveh and these poor souls don't know *who* they should be repenting to? How is it that Jonah's self-centered religiosity has so insulated him from his target audience that he doesn't even notice that he hasn't clarified who the God of Israel is?

I see Jonah in action here and I fear that I see too much of Christ's church. How much effort are we going to in order to communicate the character of our God to our communities? How would you characterize your church? "Us four, no more"? Or perhaps "Christ's Country Club"? Or maybe "No worries, any god will do!" Is your Sunday gathering one in which a seeker can count on a welcome? Will that seeker *ever* get past greeting time and be included in a meaningful conversation with someone in your congregation? Or do you find yourself every spring at the high school graduation celebration with *every* twelfth-grader on the platform speaking of how they've been raised in this church and that's why they are here? Perhaps even more challenging, does your Sunday sermon *actually* communicate the gospel? Or have you settled for a non-threatening, culturally acceptable moralism garbed in a Bible verse? (We in the guild call that sort of message representative of the MTD religion: "Moral, therapeutic deism." MTD is the religion that many churches have embraced in the name of Christianity. A religion that is interested in the idea that there is a God, that people should act morally, and we should work toward therapeutically healing ourselves, but one that is not at all interested in a God who defines himself and places non-negotiable expectations on his people. In our story, the sailors and the Ninevites were ready to meet Yahweh . . . but there was no one interested in making his character known.

An Angry Prophet

First Contact

Warning: flammable questions ahead. Do you watch CNN? Or Fox News? Do you think God is a Democrat? Or is he a Republican? Is there an American flag hanging in your church sanctuary? And how do you feel when asked to recite the Pledge of Allegiance? How would you identify Malcolm X—hero or villain? Do you live in northern California (Jefferson) or SoCal? Which one was the patriot, Grant or Lee? All of these questions touch on the red-hot button of how close you equate your *faith* with your *nation*. Do *not* try these questions at your next family gathering.

Into the Book

Now we get to see how Jonah responds to God's compassion toward the Ninevites. Starting with Jonah 4:1 we reconnect with our main human character. Jonah has actually been off-stage from 3:5–3:10, during which time we've witnessed the commendable pliancy of the Ninevites. The Ninevites have been able to embrace their own fallenness and begged a God they do not yet know for forgiveness. Let's see if our prophet does as well.

Jonah 4:1-5

¹But this was very displeasing to Jonah, and he became angry. ²He prayed to the LORD and said, "O LORD! Is not this what I said while I was still in my own country? That is why I fled to Tarshish at the beginning; for I knew that you are a gracious God and merciful, slow to anger, and abounding in steadfast love, and ready to relent from punishing. ³And now, O LORD, please take my life from me, for it is better for me to die than to live." ⁴And the LORD said, "Is it right for you to be angry?" ⁵Then Jonah went out of the city and sat down east of the city, and made a booth for himself there. He sat under it in the shade, waiting to see what would become of the city. (NRSV)

- If possible, read verse 1 in several different translations. What are some other renderings for "very displeasing"?

- Why was Jonah angry?

- Highlight what Jonah says he knows of the character of God.

- What does he ask God to do to him?

- Why do you think Jonah would rather die than live?

- What is Jonah waiting for in verse 5? What do you think Jonah was expecting to "become of the city"?

Most folks know the story of the good Samaritan found in Luke 10:30–37. In this parable, Jesus draws on the well-known reputation of the fourteen-mile road from Jerusalem to Jericho ("the red road" possibly "the way of blood"). He taps into three equally well-known characters in his world: the priest (a highly educated professional and influential holy man), a Levite (a more blue-collar holy man), and a Samaritan (the despised other in the first-century Jewish world). Know that the journey between Jerusalem and

Jericho is fairly short, but it passes through the sparsely populated and water-less territory of the Judean wilderness, and the descent from Jerusalem to Jericho is 3,300 feet!

Luke 10:30-37

[30]Jesus replied with a story: "A Jewish man was traveling from Jerusalem down to Jericho, and he was attacked by bandits. They stripped him of his clothes, beat him up, and left him half dead beside the road.

[31]"By chance a priest came along. But when he saw the man lying there, he crossed to the other side of the road and passed him by. [32]A [Levite] walked over and looked at him lying there, but he also passed by on the other side.

[33]"Then a despised Samaritan came along, and when he saw the man, he felt compassion for him. [34]Going over to him, the Samaritan soothed his wounds with olive oil and wine and bandaged them. Then he put the man on his own donkey and took him to an inn, where he took care of him. [35]The next day he handed the innkeeper two silver coins, telling him, 'Take care of this man. If his bill runs higher than this, I'll pay you the next time I'm here.'

[36]"Now which of these three would you say was a neighbor to the man who was attacked by bandits?" Jesus asked.

[37]The man replied, "The one who showed him mercy."

Then Jesus said, "Yes, now go and do the same." (NLT)

- What was the ethnicity of the travelling man who was assaulted by robbers?

- Who do you think those robbers might have been?

- What are some *rational* reasons why the priest and Levite didn't stop to help the injured man?

- What might be some less rational, or at least less noble, reasons why the priest and the Levite didn't stop?

- What do you know about Samaritans and why they might have been despised in Jesus' day?

- When Jesus makes this Samaritan the hero, how do you think Jesus' audience responds?

- When the Samaritan stops, and puts his own resources on the line to help, Jesus identifies him as what?

- Both the Samaritan and Jesus' audience will have to overcome their own biases and nationalism to be able to truly take part in this story. How does the way Jesus tells the story help his audience to do that?

- What do you think Jonah would need to help him identify the Ninevites as neighbor?

Real People, Real Places, Real Faith

Nationalism is nothing new. In fact, if your group has already worked through *Epic of Eden: Understanding the Old Testament*, you can think of nationalism as a politicized sort of ethnocentrism. The assumption is that your national identity is normative, and everyone else's is . . . well, not normative. The sort of loyalties born of nationalism are a double-edged sword. The first edge is great—nationalism helps you know where you go, who you are, what the rules of social engagement are, and who you take care of. The second edge is not so great—identifying everyone else's nation as outside the scope of your concern, less than human, even disposable.

It is important for students of the Bible to understand that when God first revealed himself on Mount Sinai to the escaping Israelites under Moses' leadership, he revealed himself as the suzerain to their vassal nation, creating Israel as a theocracy (again, see *Epic of Eden: Understanding the Old Testament* or the InterVarsity Press publication *The Epic of Eden: A Christian*

Entry into the Old Testament). Israel rightly understood their *nation* as the kingdom of God. This means that Israel understood their political boundaries as the boundaries of the kingdom of God; and the citizens of their country as the citizens of the kingdom of God. It also means that Israel understood their political enemies as *the enemies of the kingdom of God*. Thus, it is no surprise that Jonah would start this encounter confused as to why Yahweh would be interested in the Ninevites. But as you and I know the *whole* story, we know that the character of the God of Israel is such that he will not rest until *every* son of Adam and *every* daughter of Eve is offered a road home. And if Jonah had done his homework, he would have known this as well. Take Isaiah 2:2–4 for example:

> ²It shall come to pass in the latter days that the mountain of the house of the LORD shall be established as the highest of the mountains, and shall be lifted up above the hills; and all the nations shall flow to it, ³and many peoples shall come, and say: "Come, let us go up to the mountain of the LORD, to the house of the God of Jacob, that he may teach us his ways and that we may walk in his paths." For out of Zion shall go the law, and the word of the LORD from Jerusalem. ⁴He shall judge between the nations, and shall decide disputes for many peoples; and they shall beat their swords into plowshares, and their spears into pruning hooks; nation shall not lift up sword against nation, neither shall they learn war anymore. (ESV)

All this to say, we should not be surprised that Jonah had merged his faith with his nationalism. But we should be surprised that after his underwater education, Jonah preferred to hang onto his own very limited worldview than embrace that of his God. All said, we should be surprised that Jonah could not see in the faces of the Ninevites the lost children of Adam.

Our People, Our Places, Our Faith

In his book on the medieval rabbis and their commentary on the book of Jonah, Rabbi Steven Bob makes the statement that when God asks, "Why are you upset about this?" God is not simply inquiring into Jonah's emotional state. Rather, he is expressing his amazement at Jonah's self-centered attitude.* Jonah was willing to risk the lives of 120,000 people so that he didn't have to cross the color line. Jonah was willing to sacrifice the lives of 120,000 people to prove he was right. Jonah, who had been rescued from certain death in the gentle jaws of an obedient whale, was still more upset about the untimely death of a castor oil plant than 120,000 humans and countless livestock. In the privacy of your own heart, ask yourself if your nationalism/self-absorption has blinded you to the real needs of the people around you. Where have you preferred to be right and/or comfortable over the holy? Who in your world have you identified simply by their national/political identity and allowed yourself to villainize an entire collection of humanity by a single label? Who have you identified as disposable?

---

*Steven Bob, *Go to Nineveh: Medieval Jewish Commentaries on the Book of Jonah* (Eugene, OR: Pickwick Publications, 2013), 38.

No Servant Is above His Master

First Contact

> Vengeance is not the point; change is. But the trouble is that in most people's minds the thought of victory and the thought of punishing the enemy coincide.
>
> —Barbara Deming

Into the Book

There are some very telling comparisons between Jonah's story and that of Moses in Exodus 32:30–34:8. Moses' story follows directly after the infamous golden calf episode at the base of Mount Sinai. You remember, the one where Israel decided to make their own god in their own image and ditch the God who had just delivered them from Egypt because Moses had taken too long up there on top of the mountain? Obviously, this incident led to tremendous suffering and conflict, and in his exasperation,

Yahweh declared that he would wipe out the Israelites and start again with Moses.

Real People, Real Places, Real Faith

As we discussed in the first video lecture, the office of the prophet in Israel is modeled off of Moses' role at Mount Sinai. As we learned, in Exodus 20:18–19, Israel begged Moses to be the mediator between them (at the foot of the mountain) and God (all fiery and thunderous at the top of the mountain). The people said: "*You* speak to us, and we will listen. But don't let God speak directly to us, or we will die!" (v. 19 NLT, emphasis added). So Moses did as he was asked, and this role of divine mediator and diplomat became the job description of the office of the prophet in Israel. God spoke to the prophet in the privacy of the divine council, and the prophet carried that word to the people. This was Jonah's job description. And, of course, Jonah's primary role model in that occupation was Moses himself.

We know from 2 Kings 14:23–29 that Jonah was well aware of what it meant to be a prophet in Israel's theocracy. He had served his function by speaking to Jeroboam II and rightly predicted Yahweh's actions on behalf of his people. And, interestingly, Jonah had served God's kingdom rightly under a very wicked Israelite king (Jeroboam II). Yet in the juncture we investigated, Jonah failed to mimic the most important part of Moses' character—his adaptation of his own character to the character of his God. As a result, when Yahweh was ready to wipe out the Israelites, *Moses* actually reminded *Yahweh* who he is. As the title of this study communicates, a slave is not above his master; and so Moses would not behave in a fashion that he knew contradicted Yahweh's character. Likewise, Jonah's role was to be the representative of Yahweh; to be his deployed diplomat to a human ruler. In our narrative, Yahweh had sent his diplomat to the lord of Nineveh. And although Jonah had not gone so far as to *change* Yahweh's message, he sure wasn't happy about it. And rather than investing his energy in bringing the Ninevites to a place where they understood his Master, Jonah spent his best energy *arguing* with his Master.

Exodus	Exodus Questions
32:9-10, 31-32 ⁹"I have seen these people," the LORD said to Moses, "and they are a stiff-necked people. ¹⁰Now leave me alone so that my anger may burn against them and that I may destroy them. Then I will make you into a great nation." . . . ³¹So Moses went back to the LORD and said, "Oh, what a great sin these people have committed! They have made themselves gods of gold. ³²But now, please forgive their sin—but if not, then blot me out of the book you have written." *Yahweh commanded Moses to make a second set of tablets so that he could start this covenant thing again. Moses did what he was told . . . and God showed up. This is what Yahweh had to say about himself.* **34:6-7** ⁶Then the LORD passed by in front of him and proclaimed, "The LORD, the LORD God, compassionate and gracious, slow to anger, and abounding in lovingkindness and truth; ⁷who keeps lovingkindness for thousands, who forgives iniquity, transgression and sin; yet He will by no means leave the guilty unpunished, visiting the iniquity of fathers on the children and on the grandchildren to the third and fourth generations." [NASB]	Underline how God described the Israelites. What did Yahweh intend to do to them? Highlight what Moses asked God to do to him. After all Moses had been through with these folks, were you surprised by his generous and self-sacrificial response? Underline the modifiers (adjectives) that God used to describe himself. Compare these modifiers to those he used to describe the Israelites above.

Jonah	Jonah Questions
3:10–4:5 ¹⁰When God saw what they had done and how they had put a stop to their evil ways, he changed his mind and did not carry out the destruction he had threatened.	Circle Jonah's responses to Yahweh's reprieve regarding wiping out the Ninevites.
⁴:¹This change of plans greatly upset Jonah, and he became very angry. ²So he complained to the LORD about it: "Didn't I say before I left home that you would do this, LORD? That is why I ran away to Tarshish! I knew that you are a merciful and compassionate God, slow to get angry and filled with unfailing love. You are eager to turn back from destroying people. ³Just kill me now, LORD! I'd rather be dead than alive if what I predicted will not happen."	Using the same color that you used for Moses, highlight what Jonah asked God to do to him. How does Jonah's request to die differ from Moses' request? Underline the parallels you see in Yahweh's description of himself in Exodus 34:6-7 and Jonah's complaint in Jonah 4:2.
⁴The LORD replied, "Is it right for you to be angry about this?"	Should Jonah be *complaining* that his God is gracious?
⁵Then Jonah went out to the east side of the city and made a shelter to sit under as he waited to see what would happen to the city. [NLT]	What sort of assumptions must Jonah have been carrying around regarding the Ninevites if he thought that Yahweh's disposition toward them was a problem? What sort of assumptions must Jonah have been carrying around regarding his own character if he was finding God's behavior a problem? What do you think would motivate Jonah to say: "I'd rather be dead than alive if what I predicted will not happen." [4:3 NLT]

Our People, Our Places, Our Faith

We have got to assume that Jonah was trained in orthodoxy—that means he had been trained in "right doctrine." And with the help of a cyclone and a cetacean, Jonah had learned orthopraxis—that means "right practice." But we come all the way to chapter 4 and see that Jonah has yet to learn orthopathos—"right feeling." The entire point of the gospel is to make the identity of God known so that the sinner can reconcile with their Creator and be transformed back into the image of the One who made that sinner-now-saint in the first place. The transformation that *should* come from right doctrine (knowing who God actually is) is a resurrected heart (orthopathos), which longs to follow right practice (orthopraxis). In other words, orthodoxy is supposed to result in orthopathos, which naturally brings about orthopraxis. That's the nature of redemption. But that wasn't the case for Jonah. And, to be really honest, I would say the same is true for many who call themselves "Christian." They've been raised on the gospel, but the gospel hasn't changed them at all. Their practice still springs from whatever keeps them most comfortable and the cultural norms around them. Their hearts are still not a reflection of the heart of their God (cf. Romans 8:29). How can someone *know* the gospel so well and not have been changed by it at all? We could ask Jonah. But it would be better to ask ourselves.

Does Jonah Get It?

A Word from the Author

On February 21, 2018, the world lost one of the greatest spokesmen for the gospel that it has ever seen, William Franklin Graham. Born on November 7, 1918, this broadly acclaimed religious leader and statesman lived for ninety-nine years. In that time, he was the confidant and counselor to presidents and kings, spoke to nearly 215 million people in more than 185 countries and territories, and advised hundreds of millions more through television, video, film, books, and webcasts. As any clergyperson will tell you, Billy Graham's messages were simple. But his impact was almost unfathomable. What did he do that others had not? Many would say that one thing Reverend Graham did right is that he kept the main thing (the gospel) the main thing.

Many would also note his uncompromised integrity, which allowed the world to see at least one Christian leader who seemed to really mean it. Longtime *Time* contributors Nancy Gibbs and Michael Duffy, coauthors of *The Preacher and the Presidents: Billy Graham in the White House,* say that Graham regularly insisted that his crusades be audited and made public to avoid any hint of scandal. "He was turning down million-dollar television and Hollywood offers half a century ago," Gibbs and Duffy wrote in *Time* in 2007. "If he had wanted to get rich, he could have been many, many times over."* He was also known for his deep respect and fidelity to his wife, a commitment that manifested itself in many ways, one of which was to *never* stay in a hotel room without another male staff person present so that there was no opportunity for sexual compromise.

But perhaps the thing Graham *should* be best known for is that his crusades never began or ended simply when he arrived and departed. Rather, each crusade began months prior when local Christians were deployed to pray and organize in preparation for the public event. And each crusade continued long after the event was over, as area church members and pastors responded to the thousands who came forward with outreach and *discipleship*. A one-time commitment at an emotionally charged event does not a Christian make. Neither does a one-time act of repentance on the streets of Nineveh.

The last question I will be asking as we approach our last week of study together is this: What might have happened in Jonah's world if our statesman/religious leader had thought in terms of *discipleship* not just *conversion*?

Real Time and Space

When Jonah leaves Nineveh and heads home, he will return to a country that is generally prosperous and at peace. As we have discussed several times, the first half of the eighth century is a time of economic expansion, alliance, and peace for the Northern Kingdom. This is true largely because a dark age has engulfed Assyria in an era of stagnation and decline and therefore made space for Israel and Judah to thrive. This era of decline in Assyria will begin to retreat with the rise of Tiglath-Pileser III in 745 BCE. Under this exceptionally capable leader, a new chapter begins for the ancient

*Nancy Gibbs and Michael Duffy, "Why Christopher Hitchens Is Wrong about Billy Graham," *Time Magazine,* September 18, 2007.

empire. Naming himself the "King of Sumer and Akkad," Tiglath-Pileser will reorganize and redeploy a dying empire as an expressly efficient military machine and begin to annex territories west of the Euphrates for the first time in Assyrian history. Thus, with the onset of Tiglath-Pileser's success, we witness the onset of Israel's decline.

By the end of his reign, Tiglath-Pileser's list of conquered provinces and tributary regions will include Aram-Damascus, the coastal cities of Phoenicia, Israel, Judah, Gaza, Ammon, Moab, and Edom. As we learned in the *Epic of Eden: Isaiah*, this voracious Assyrian king will actually be *invited* into several of these relationships—not the least being the once independent nation of Judah under King Ahaz. This means that under Tiglath-Pileser, Assyria will gain all the access it needs to control the international highways and reach its true prize—Egypt. With Assyria's coffers overflowing at home from tribute and trade, a centralized command economy emerges facilitated by a very impressive road and messaging network. These resources result in an unprecedented and ever-expanding military force, a seemingly unhindered journey toward world domination, and what some identify as the *pax Assyria*. In 734–732 BCE this expansion results in the Syro-Ephraimite Wars that topple Aram-Damascus and reduce both Israel and Judah to Assyrian provinces. By 722 BCE this expansion wipes out the Northern Kingdom, displacing the northern tribes from their homeland *forever*. By 701 BCE Assyria reaches Judah, leaving King Hezekiah on his face begging God to deliver his besieged capital from the iron fist of the newest Assyrian king, Sennacherib (2 Kings 18–19). By 671 BCE, Esarhaddon will conquer Egypt.

But, of course, Jonah doesn't know any of this. Rather, he is somewhere in the "well, that's over" zone, and having managed to survive his anomalous calling to preach to the Ninevites is apparently settling back into life as usual back at home. We hear nothing more from Jonah. And based on the ending of his book, we really don't know where his heart landed in the end. It seems that this prophet has little enthusiasm for his outrageously successful preaching to one of the oldest empires on earth, and less concern for the tens of thousands who responded. Rather, after a revival that should have rocked the world, Jonah heads home and does . . . nothing.

"Woe to Those Who Call Evil Good, and Good Evil"*

First Contact

"I've learned a lot about good and evil. They are not always what they appear to be." These are the words of Charles Van Doren, the uniquely gifted, but completely compromised star of the 1950's quiz show *Twenty-One*. When the intrigue over his winning streak reached the level of a congressional investigation, and it became apparent that the producers had been giving Van Doren the answers before the show, Van Doren apologized in disgrace. He spoke of how the producers had convinced him that by appearing on a nationally televised program and winning he was doing a great service to teachers and to education by increasing public respect for the work of educators everywhere. He spoke of how he *wanted* to believe them, and in his desire he was seduced into actions of which he was now ashamed. Good and evil . . . they are not always what they appear to be.

---

*Isaiah 5:20 (NASB)

Into the Book

As mentioned in the video lesson, the word "evil" (Hebrew *rā'āh*, sometimes translated "wickedness" or "calamity") shows up a good bit in the book of Jonah. And I'm pretty convinced that our narrator wants us to see, like Van Doren states, that evil isn't always what it appears to be. Moreover, I think our narrator wants to demonstrate that what Jonah thinks is evil, looks pretty different from what Yahweh thinks is evil.

Read each of the following passages. The italicized words indicate the English translation of *rā'āh*. Write in the word your Bible uses for *rā'āh* in the second column. In the third, identify exactly what is being identified as evil.

Evil in the book of Jonah	Your Bible's translation of *rā'āh*	What is being identified as evil?
Jonah 1:2 "their *wickedness* has come up before me" [NRSV]		
Jonah 1:7 "this *calamity* has struck us" [NASB]		
Jonah 3:8 "the *evil* that is in their hands" [author's paraphrase]		
Jonah 3:10 Then God relented concerning the *calamity* which He had declared He would bring upon them. [NASB]		
Jonah 4:1 But it *greatly displeased* Jonah and he became angry. [NASB]		

Jonah 4:2 "for I knew that You are a gracious and compassionate God, slow to anger and abundant in lovingkindness, and one who relents concerning *calamity*." [NASB]		
Jonah 4:6 So the LORD God appointed a plant and it grew up over Jonah to be a shade over his head to deliver him from his *discomfort*. And Jonah was extremely happy about the plant. [NASB]		

- Highlight the evils in this list you would naturally identify as evil.

- Now underline the evils in this list you would naturally identify as trivial.

- What did God think was evil here and what did Jonah think was evil?

Real People, Real Places, Real Faith

What does a community's definition of good and evil have to say about them? Most would say *a lot*. Unlike the law code of most nations, Israel's definition of good and evil came from the self-revelation of their God as articulated in the covenant. Thus, the laws of Israel were not manmade laws, they were the result of the Creator of the cosmos condescending to express himself in the midst of a particular time and place and call a particular people to live in a fashion that portrayed him to the world. Repeatedly Israel is spoken of as a light to the nations and/or a witness to the Gentiles—this is because in living out the covenant they were actually displaying the character of God to a broken and fallen world.

It is important for us to realize that God's definition of good and evil is in no way arbitrary. Rather, as is clear from the challenge of the tree of the knowledge of good and evil in the garden, to the New Testament command to be "conformed to the image of the Son" (Rom. 8:29), God's definition of good is coming from his own character. So as we consider the Ten Commandments of the Old Testament, we are not simply interacting with a utilitarian social code designed to keep order. We are interacting with a real space and time description of the character of God himself. For this reason, those who call good evil are committing a crime far worse than category confusion. They are attempting to redefine the character of God; to make him in their own image. And they are doing so based on their supposedly superior understanding of what good should be. In other words, these folks who attempt to redefine God's definition of good as evil or vice versa are making their *own* character the paradigm . . . they are making themselves god. This is why the crime in the garden was such a big deal. This is why breaking the Sinai covenant was such a big deal. This is why Jonah's unwillingness to celebrate God's purposes with the Ninevites is such a big deal.

Our People, Our Places, Our Faith

As an educator in a Christian college, I often meet students who are third and fourth generation offspring of a family that is broadly known for their Christian commitments. As a result of the family's heritage, these kids wind up in my classroom. But often I find that these kids with long lines of faith and service in their own backgrounds are the ones who are struggling the most with their own commitment to Christ. Why? Well there can be lots of answers to that question, but one of them is that they have too often been raised in an environment where what I would call the peripheral rules of church culture have superseded the essence of real Christian discipleship. These would be the kids who think that denying the deity of Christ is okay, but smoking a cigarette will send them directly to hell. This is the adolescent girl who is raped, winds up pregnant, and sent away alone to complete her pregnancy, give birth, and place the baby for adoption so that her missionary parents are not yanked out of their missionary posts by the

"Christian" leaders and constituency who have placed them there. These are the kids who have been awarded positions of leadership over and over again because of their lineage, but have never been asked (or held accountable to) the essential questions of conversion and sanctification themselves. These are often kids who have lived with an unending display of hypocrisy in their own homes, so they have learned to play the same game. In other words, these are kids who have been taught by example to call good evil, and evil good. What happens to these kids? We usually lose them. Why? Well, why in the world should they stick around in a world where playing the game has become a synonym for being Christian? As we ponder our own lives, families, youth groups, and elder boards . . . what definition of good and evil are we displaying with our *lives*? Are we allowing Christianity to (re)define our communities? Or are we allowing our communities to redefine Christianity?

DAY TWO

Yahweh Appoints a Plant, a Worm, and a Wind

First Contact

"Hypocrisy is the homage vice pays to virtue."—Francois de La Rochefoucauld

Into the Book

Now we get to the central message of the book. Our literary theme is "to appoint" (Hebrew *mānāh*).

Jonah 4:6-8

6So the LORD God appointed a plant and it grew up over Jonah to be a shade over his head to deliver him from his discomfort. And Jonah was extremely happy about the plant. 7But God appointed a worm when dawn came the next day and it attacked the plant and it withered. 8When the sun came up God appointed a scorching east wind, and the sun beat down on Jonah's head so that he became faint and begged with *all* his soul to die, saying, "Death is better to me than life." (NASB)

■ Highlight everything in these verses that God "appointed."

■ What are Jonah's responses to these things God appointed?

■ What would you say is the real reason that Jonah stated "Death is better to me than life"?

■ The only other passage in the book where God "appoints" is in Jonah 1:17: "And the LORD *appointed* a great fish to swallow Jonah, and Jonah was in the stomach of the fish three days and three nights" (NASB, emphasis mine).

■ Adding Jonah 1:17 to your list, list here everything God has appointed in this book. How would you classify these things?

■ What does the fact that God can appoint all these different sorts of creatures/plants/things to do his will tell us about God's sovereignty?

■ Now ponder the fact that one unspoken in this story is that God had also appointed Jonah to do as he said and go to Nineveh. Which of these characters that God had appointed failed to do as they were told?

Jonah 4:9-11

⁹Then God said to Jonah, "Do you have good reason to be angry about the plant?" And he said, "I have good reason to be angry, even to death." ¹⁰Then the LORD said, "You had compassion on the plant for which you did not work

and which you did not cause to grow, which came up overnight and perished overnight. [11]Should I not have compassion on Nineveh, the great city in which there are more than 120,000 persons who do not know the difference between their right and left hand, as well as many animals?" (NASB)

■ Underline the question God asked Jonah and circle Jonah's response.

■ How would you describe God's posture/attitude in this exchange with Jonah?

■ How would you describe Jonah's posture/attitude in this exchange?

■ Placing the plant and the Ninevites side by side, why was the latter more important in God's government than the plant? Don't just give the easy answer that they are human—what other reasons are offered in chapter 4?

■ What do you think God's pedagogical plan was? In other words, why did God choose *this* method (the exercise with the plant, the worm, and the wind) to get past Jonah's hard heart?

■ What was it that God wanted Jonah to understand? Teachers in the crowd, what was the learning objective here?

Real People, Real Places, Real Faith

I honestly struggle to imagine a man of Jonah's stature parked outside of Nineveh, huddled under a homemade lean-to, assaulted by an east wind, burning under the Mesopotamian sun, grumbling about his castor oil plant dying, eagerly watching for Yahweh to rain down fire and brimstone on the inhabitants of Nineveh. This picture of a prophet doesn't work for me. It doesn't work because I know about Samuel who grieved Saul's failures,

Isaiah who *begged* for his people to repent, Jeremiah the "weeping prophet" who chose to stay in the path of danger in Jerusalem when he knew full well his congregation was *never* going to listen to him and Nebuchadnezzar II was on his way. Yet it seems that our man of God was indeed an obstinate, self-absorbed bigot. What do I do with that?

I often speak of how our biblical characters were not ivory-tower people. They were *real* people. And perhaps this reality is no more apparent than right here in Jonah 4. This real guy was actually more concerned about his sun exposure than he was about 120,000 human lives. This officer of Israel's theocracy, this representative of the divine council, was actually more concerned about his own comfort than the human beings who had responded to his message. Could it be true that his only response to Nineveh's repentance was to go sit east of the city in order to watch the live coverage of the supernatural disaster awaiting them? Oh. My. Goodness. Where could such callous hypocrisy in a man entrusted with the word of God come from? And then I think of Yahweh . . . who went to the trouble of creating an object lesson for his prodigal prophet. An object lesson that would (hopefully) reach beyond Jonah's self-absorption and get him thinking about *real* suffering, real people, and what real death for this city would look like. Did it work? Man . . . I sure hope so.

Our People, Our Places, Our Faith

This lesson began with a famous quote about hypocrisy. If you were to ask a random person on the street the number-one reason they no longer go to church, the answer would be "Christians." Not the Christians who launched the abolitionist movement or women's suffrage. Not the Christians who have built the hospitals and orphanages sprinkled across this world in the name of the gospel. Not the Amy Carmichaels or the Joyce Chellises, not the Neil and Danielle Carlstroms. I'm fairly confident these folks are not our problem. Rather, the main reason the unsaved have no interest in church is because of the systemic hypocrisy within our faith communities. Our communities who have chosen to define Christianity by our own comfort zone, as opposed to allowing our own comfort zone to be redefined by Christ. Jonah, huddled against Yahweh's east wind on the borders of Nineveh, is nearly a caricature of the sort of blind, calloused hypocrisy that the world sees when it sees us. I say, let's show them something different. Let's show them Jesus.

What If?

First Contact

In our video lecture this week I am going to pursue the "What If?" game. *What if* Jonah had headed home from Nineveh bubbling over with the story of how Yahweh had actually broken through the harsh exterior of the arrogant Assyrians and they had repented! *What if* Jonah had shared this story with the like-minded of his community and they had all concluded that this unprecedented event needed some follow-up? *What if* these same leaders of the faith community had decided—similar to a Billy Graham crusade—that the Nineveh crusade wasn't over until discipleship had been deployed? What if?

Into the Book

The book of Acts records the acts of the early church and the spread of the gospel in "Jerusalem, and in all Judea and Samaria, and to the ends of the earth" (Acts 1:8). Beginning in chapter 13 and continuing throughout the remainder of the book, the focus of the book of Acts is Paul and his missionary journeys. What can we learn from Paul about follow-up?

Acts 18:19-26

¹⁹⁻²¹They landed in Ephesus, where Priscilla and Aquila got off and stayed. Paul left the ship briefly to go to the meeting place and preach to the Jews. They wanted him to stay longer, but he said he couldn't. But after saying good-bye, he promised, "I'll be back, God willing."

²¹⁻²²From Ephesus he sailed to Caesarea. He greeted the church there, and then went on to Antioch, completing the journey.

²³After spending a considerable time with the Antioch Christians, Paul set off again for Galatia and Phrygia, retracing his old tracks, one town after another, putting fresh heart into the disciples.

²⁴⁻²⁶A man named Apollos came to Ephesus. He was a Jew, born in Alexandria, Egypt, and a terrific speaker, eloquent and powerful in his preaching of the Scriptures. He was well-educated in the way of the Master and fiery in his enthusiasm. Apollos was accurate in everything he taught about Jesus up to a point, but he only went as far as the baptism of John. He preached with power in the meeting place. When Priscilla and Aquila heard him, they took him aside and told him the rest of the story. (MSG)

- Priscilla and Aquila were Jewish believers in the church at Corinth where Paul had spent a year and a half evangelizing and discipling the community there (see Acts 18:1–11). Why do you think Paul left Priscilla and Aquila in Ephesus?

- Underline all of the places Paul went after he left Ephesus.

- Circle what Paul did in Galatia and Phrygia.

- Circle the things that Priscilla and Aquila did when they heard Apollos speaking in the synagogue.

If we continue reading in the book of Acts, we see that Paul *returned* to Ephesus *again . . .*

Acts 19:1-7, 10

[1]While Apollos was at Corinth, Paul took the road through the interior and arrived at Ephesus. There he found some disciples [2]and asked them, "Did you receive the Holy Spirit when you believed?"

They answered, "No, we have not even heard that there is a Holy Spirit."
[3]So Paul asked, "Then what baptism did you receive?"
"John's baptism," they replied.

[4]Paul said, "John's baptism was a baptism of repentance. He told the people to believe in the one coming after him, that is, in Jesus." [5]On hearing this, they were baptized in the name of the Lord Jesus. [6]When Paul placed his hands on them, the Holy Spirit came on them, and they spoke in tongues and prophesied. [7]There were about twelve men in all. . . .

[10]This went on for two years, so that all the Jews and Greeks who lived in the province of Asia heard the word of the Lord.

- Knowing that biblical narrative is very economical (a.k.a. "sometimes overly succinct"), what is the first thing our narrator tells us that Paul did when he arrived in Ephesus?

- How long did Paul remain in Ephesus?

So we've seen that Paul's strategy for evangelism in Ephesus involved visiting for the purpose of evangelism (Acts 18); leaving trained leaders in place for ongoing discipleship; returning to advance the training of the locals and the leaders; and . . . take a look at Paul's letter to the Ephesian church years later when he winds up in a prison cell in Rome.

Ephesians 1:15-19

[15]For this reason, ever since I heard about your faith in the Lord Jesus and your love for all God's people, [16]I have not stopped giving thanks for you, remembering you in my prayers. [17]I keep asking that the God of our Lord Jesus Christ, the glorious Father, may give you the Spirit of wisdom and

revelation, so that you may know him better. [18]I pray that the eyes of your heart may be enlightened in order that you may know the hope to which he has called you, the riches of his glorious inheritance in his holy people, [19]and his incomparably great power for us who believe. . . .

- Underline the specific things that Paul prayed for the Ephesians.

- What reason did Paul give for praying as he did?

- Scan the rest of Paul's letter to the Ephesians—you can just look at subtitles if your time is tight. What are the topics? In the closing of his letter, he penned these words:

Ephesians 6:21-22

[21]Tychicus, the dear brother and faithful servant in the Lord, will tell you everything, so that you also may know how I am and what I am doing. [22]I am sending him to you for this very purpose, that you may know how we are, and that he may encourage you.

- Why did Paul send Tychicus to the Ephesians? How did Paul, even in his absence, ensure that the Ephesians would continue to be discipled?

Look at the opening line of the epistle to Timothy:

1 Timothy 1:1-3

[1]Paul, an apostle of Christ Jesus according to the commandment of God our Savior, and of Christ Jesus, who is our hope,

[2]To Timothy, my true child in the faith: Grace, mercy, and peace from God the Father and Christ Jesus our Lord.

[3]As I urged you upon my departure for Macedonia remain on at Ephesus in order that you may instruct . . . (NASB)

- Who was this letter addressed to?

- Where did this pastor serve?

- Who trained Timothy to be a pastor?

- Looking at Paul's efforts here, and knowing that we likely only have a representative number of those efforts, how many touches does it take to lead a new convert into the place of disciple? How many more touches do you think it takes to produce a Priscilla, an Aquila, a Tychicus, or a Timothy?

Real People, Real Places, Real Faith

Have you ever heard of a Levite? The Levites were part of Israel's priestly caste. As you know, the priests of Israel were tasked with mediating for the people of God as they came to meet Yahweh in worship. The entire tribe of Levi was "set apart" for this task following the golden calf incident at Sinai (Exod. 32:26–29). The priests' job description included collecting tithes and offerings, assisting in sacrifice, leading in prayer and liturgy, and keeping the house of God in order. What you might not know is that there were two categories of priests: the Aaronic priests and the Levites. All of these representatives of Israel's cult (i.e., religious system) came from the tribe of Levi, but the sons of Aaron had the particular privilege of always serving in the temple (or tabernacle before there was a temple) and serving in the role of high priest.

The Levites were a more generic class of priest—the folks responsible for the grunt labor of actually raising, lowering, and transporting the tabernacle, transporting the ark, and cleaning up the precinct that was regularly exposed to lots of humans, animals, and animal slaughter (see Numbers 1:47–53; 3:25–37). They also served in the central precinct of the temple on a rotating basis, but when they were off duty were scattered throughout the land. This is because unlike the other tribes of Israel, the Levites were not assigned a specific territory. Rather, forty-eight cities with their pasturelands were given to Levites (see Numbers 35:1–8). These cities were gifted by each tribe, with the larger tribes being expected to give more than the smaller tribes. And in this fashion, the Levites—specialists in God's law—were scattered throughout the land (see Genesis 49:5–7; Deuteronomy 33:8–9). The idea here is that these representatives of the covenant were sprinkled like leaven (or salt or light?) throughout the territories and thereby brought the testimony of the covenant to every corner of Israel.

The Levites are instructed in Deuteronomy 33:10 to instruct the people in the law. In other words, our Levites become something akin to the local parson. A local expert in the law of God; a local leader in the task of discipleship. Of additional interest is that in payment for their service (and in recognition of their landlessness), Deuteronomy commands that the Levites be regularly supported by the local populace with tithes and gifts and invitations to the family table. In fact, the Levite appears regularly in the list of the marginalized in Israel: "the widow, the orphan, the refugee, and the Levite" (Deuteronomy 14:29; 16:11, 14; 26:12–15). Keep that one in mind when you think of your youth pastor and Sunday school superintendent!

Our People, Our Places, Our Faith

Rabbi Steven Bob concludes his study on the book of Jonah with the following:

> The book of Jonah ends abruptly without telling us Jonah's response to God's lesson. Does Jonah learn? The sailors learned. They recognized the Eternal as the ruler of the universe. They made vows and sacrifices. The people of Nineveh learned. They repented for their sins and turned to God. Does Jonah learn? Is Jonah going to walk with God? By not answering this question the author allows us to place ourselves into the

story at the end. The real question facing us as we conclude the book of Jonah is did *we* learn? Are we going to follow the examples of the sailors and the Ninevites by turning to God? Or will we remain self-absorbed like Jonah?*

I can't think of a better place to end this book. Jonah was a good man. He was a moral man. A faithful church-goer, he was even educated and a patriot. And yet he did not understand the character of the God he served. He thought his God was limited, and therefore he could run away from his calling. He thought his God was vengeful, and therefore he was going to drown in the sea. He thought his God was irrelevant, and therefore was sending him on an absurd mission. Moreover, Jonah thought that his God (like him) did not care about the 120,000 lost souls of Nineveh—because the Ninevites weren't like him. Most interesting to me is that Jonah did not seem to think that the conversion of the Ninevites *had anything to do with him*. Jonah would learn very differently during the Syro-Ephraimite Wars of 734–732 BCE and then in 722 BCE when the revived Assyrian Empire ravaged his land and his people, leaving the ten northern tribes nothing but a memory and his home territory of Zebulun a no-man's land (see Isaiah 9:1). We the reader will learn that on all these fronts Jonah was wrong. And there is some part of our minds that is still shouting, "Jonah, how could you?"

But Yahweh had a different approach. Rather than tossing his servant aside, Yahweh chose to correct, to rehabilitate, to reeducate, and to send Jonah out again. And although we cannot be clear as to how Jonah responded to the last question his God posed to him at the end of the book, we are very clear on one thing: Yahweh is indeed the God of second chances. So how about you? Do you think that your God is limited? Do you think he is vengeful? How about irrelevant or uninvested? Wrong on all fronts. Do you think you've used up your last second chance? Wrong again. And what about the conversion of the souls to the left and right of you . . . well, if there is nothing else we've learned from Jonah's book, it has *everything* to do with us.

---

*Steven Bob, *Go to Nineveh: Medieval Jewish Commentaries on the Book of Jonah* (Eugene, OR: Pickwick Publications, 2013), 159.

Group Session/
Leader's Guide

AN INTRODUCTION FOR GROUP LEADERS

Logistics

Each member of your group should receive a copy of *The Epic of Eden: Jonah*. It is intended to provide each participant with homework that helps them prepare for the next group gathering where the videos are to be shown. Just to be clear, there is no preparatory work for the first week, but from that week forward there is work to be done in the study guide to get ready for the next week's session. Each week has three sets of exercises; our thought is that finding three slots of time per week to prepare this homework is a reasonable expectation—not too much, not too little. But also *please* communicate to your group members that homework is *not required*. There will be plenty to do and talk about even if some of your members never crack the cover of their study guides. Also know that these studies are intended to help your members to enter into the inductive study of their Bibles.

Each week of home studies commences with "A Word from the Author" introducing the topic and a short section situating the week's study in "Real Time and Space." After those introductory pieces, each daily study begins with a section titled "First Contact," designed to get your members thinking about what is to come from their own real time and space. Each daily study then moves "Into the Book." This is where the inductive Bible study begins in earnest. Our primary goal is to *lead* your group members into the discovery of the Bible. The questions direct students into a close reading of the text. Next the "Real People, Real Places, Real Faith" section provides further information about the original setting of these biblical narratives and characters, and challenges your group members to get back into the Bible's real time and space—to put *themselves* into the shoes of these not-so-ivory-tower heroes. Finally, "Our People, Our Places, Our Faith" will bring the ancient story back into a contemporary setting. This exercise will help to teach your members *how* to responsibly interpret their Bible and transports texts that might have appeared irrelevant into front-and-center relevance for our contemporary contexts.

Our hope is that we've included enough different learning styles that every member of your group will find themselves engaged and challenged. As long as your members feel this way, we've succeeded.

The "Group Session Guide" (a.k.a. "Leader's Guide") is designed for you, the facilitator. If this is a home group, we recommend that an hour and a half be set aside for the video and discussion. If this is a group in a church setting, it can be modified to suit your group's schedule. In a perfect world, we recommend that the leader preview the videos. Outlines for each video session are provided for you and your group members in the "Video Notes Guide" section beginning on page 149. These are provided for you and your group members to follow along during the video as well as to provide a place for note-taking, writing down questions, and "aha" moments. Keep in mind that curriculum is a tool, not a straitjacket. *You are the leader.* You are called to lead this group. You need to adjust according to your own style. We suggest that group members be allowed to talk, ask questions, and offer their "aha" moments and personal research. These elements are critical to the success of your group. Trust your group members, trust the Bible, trust the Holy Spirit, and let your people talk. Questions are provided to facilitate the discussion.

If you've already done the other studies in the *Epic of Eden* series, then you're familiar with the format of the session guides.

As we did in the Ruth study, we have included a heading called "Launch Questions." Richter ends each of the video sessions in this study with launch questions to help your group move from spectator to participant. Those questions are included here as well. There is also a heading called "Next Week," which will provide a teaser about what is to come in the next session and help everyone stay on track.

Our prayer is that this material will give you the tools you need to successfully facilitate your group in your very own corner of the kingdom. Know that "where two or three have gathered together in My name, I am there in [your] midst" (Matt. 18:20 NASB). And know that the team behind this curriculum is praying daily that wherever you are, the Holy Spirit is with you. Godspeed!

First Things

We are including here a few *suggestions* for the group's introductory meeting. You are welcome to plan this gathering in any way that best suits your group. Let the Holy Spirit be your guide.

- Let the first gathering be mostly about the group meeting each other, getting comfortable with each other, getting the curriculum materials in hand, and getting *familiar* with those materials.
- Allow the members of the group to briefly introduce themselves (i.e., first name and in one sentence what they hope to gain from this study). If the group is more than seven, it is often good to have them turn to the person on their right and then on their left and introduce themselves before having everyone introduce to the group as a whole.
- Pass out materials and explain how the study works. Actually *show* them the various sections of a day's study. Make sure they are clear that the homework is to be completed *before* the video for each week. (The participants should work on Week Two at home prior to viewing the Session 2 video at your next gathering, and so on.)
- Turn to the Introduction session on page 132 for facilitating the discussion for this introductory session and view "Introduction" (located on disc 1). Know that the first (introductory) video is briefer than the rest (5 minutes) in order to provide your group the time it needs for all the logistics of this first gathering. The introductory video is designed to get everyone on the same page and get everyone hooked on the book of Jonah. As you plan your schedule, it might also be a great thing to set apart a final gathering after the study is complete to debrief and celebrate with some sort of time together as a group.

Practical Tips

- Choose a space for your study that matches the size of your group, facilitates note-taking, and encourages discussion.
- Have refreshments. Lots of studies have shown that adults do way better in small groups when there are snacks available. For some reason having a cup of coffee in their hand makes it easier for adults to speak to the person next to them. And if you pass snack responsibilities around it gives everyone a chance to get involved.
- Have someone besides yourself serve as host/hostess (you've got enough to do) and think about having name tags. These are very useful for helping folks engage someone they don't really know yet and breaking down barriers.

Weekly Meeting Line Up

Debrief and Discover

This section is a break-the-ice kind of question. It is intended to get your group thinking and lead into the video for the week.

View Session # Video: "Title" (# minutes)

Each video will be approximately thirty minutes.

Launch Questions

These questions are designed to help move your group members from spectator to participant.

Dialogue and Digest

This section consists of quotes from the video with questions for discussion based on those quotes. This is also a place for group members to ask questions about the homework and share something from the homework that really captured their attention.

Decide and Do

This is the application section in which the questions are intended to move your group members to some type of action.

Next Week

Here we provide a teaser about what is to come in the next session.

Closing Prayer

This is the time to ask group members if there is something for which they would like prayer and close the session with prayer.

SESSION 1

Introduction

Debrief and Discover

What is the first thing that comes to mind when you think about the book of Jonah?

View Session 1 Video: "Introduction" (6 minutes)

The outline for this study is found on page 153 in the "Video Notes Guide" section. These are provided for you and your group members to follow along during the video as well as to provide a place for note-taking, writing down questions and "aha" moments. Have your group members turn there while watching the video.

Dialogue and Digest

Richter says: "What we're going to do is to take this book at face value. We're going to read it as one of the Prophets. We're going to recognize that Jonah himself is recognized by the canon as a minor prophet. And we are going to anticipate, at least for now, that this story actually happened and that there is something about this story that is so critical to our faith and to our understanding of the character of our God that out of everything that could have been included in the biblical text *this story* gets a place in the Minor Prophets."

- Is the idea that Jonah was a real person and that this story actually happened a new idea for you?
- How will that affect your read of the book?

Decide and Do

- Turn to the person next to you and tell them what you think will be the most challenging aspect of this study for you.

Next Week

We find the book of Jonah among the Prophets in our Bibles. Thus, we should know something about the prophetic books themselves and the office of the prophet. This is where next week's study will take us.

Closing Prayer

Ask your group members if there is something they would like prayer for—especially something highlighted by this week's video. Know that this first time you ask they might be hesitant to speak up. So be ready to model what this sort of prayer looks like.

SESSION 2

What Is a Prophet?

Debrief and Discover

If someone were to ask you to name three prophets found in the Bible could you do it? Five? Is Jonah among one of those names?

View Session 2 Video: "What Is a Prophet?" (29 minutes)

The outline for this study is found on page 155 in the "Video Notes Guide" section. Have your group members turn there while watching the video. Encourage them to take notes and jot down questions and "aha" moments.

Launch Questions

- How does this understanding of what a prophet *was* in ancient Israel affect your read of Jonah's book? How about your read of Jonah's life?
- If you could ask one question about Jonah in light of this information, what would it be?

Dialogue and Digest

- Richter provides several reasons why the book of Jonah is unique among the prophetic books of the Bible. What are those reasons?
- Which of these reasons is most intriguing to you and why?

Decide and Do

- One of the things we've learned in this lesson is that God actually speaks to the average, everyday believer and we can speak to him. What is it that you need to hear from God today? Take a moment now to tell him.

Next Week

Next week we will meet the cast of characters in our book including a prophet, a king, a nation and people known for their brutality. As we meet these characters we will get a glimpse into Jonah's world and the people to whom he is called to share the message of God's love.

Closing Prayer

Ask your group members if there is something they would like prayer for—especially something highlighted by this week's video.

Reminder: If you are behind in the reading, pick back up with Week Three, Day One tomorrow to get back on track.

The Cast of Characters: Jonah, Gath-hepher, and Jeroboam II versus the Nation of Assyria and the City of Nineveh

Debrief and Discover

As you were asked on Day Three of this week's study, can you think of one city in the world that you would avoid at all costs? What about that city would make you avoid it?

View Session 3 Video: "The Cast of Characters: Jonah, Gath-hepher, and Jeroboam II versus the Nation of Assyria and the City of Nineveh" (26 minutes)

The outline for this study is found on page 157 in the "Video Notes Guide" section. Have your group members turn there while watching the video. Encourage them to take notes and jot down questions and "aha" moments.

Launch Questions

Leaders, it is important that the following questions be asked, as they address the whole point of the book of Jonah. Answering the questions honestly can be a transformational learning moment for your group. Know that the human condition is such that we all find some "other" group of people intimidating or even distasteful. For the young African-American male, it might be a white police officer walking toward him on that empty street. For a young white man it might be the Latino clique that hangs out in the hallway between his locker and his classroom. For the Muslim mother it might be the western, white mom clique at the mall. Be sensitive to your group. Help them keep their hearts clean but open. Answer honestly . . . and think of Jonah.

- Name a group/type of people that you are afraid of. Why? Be honest.
- What do you feel when you see someone from that group walking toward you on an empty street? Standing in line behind you at a convenience store or at an airport? Knocking on your front door?

Dialogue and Digest

- Richter speaks of the brutality of the Assyrians and states that "the Assyrians themselves made kings tremble. They brag in their inscriptions about terrifying their opponents to the point where their opponents lose control of their bowels." How has this discussion, along with the images portraying their brutality, helped you to understand Jonah's decision to run the other way?

Decide and Do

- As we heard in the video, Jonah had a reason to be afraid of and even hate the very people he was called to minister to. Let's go back to our opening question for a moment. Do you have a reason to be afraid of and to hate those people in the one city you named? If you were called to minister to that city how would you respond?
- Take some time this week and throughout this study to pray for that city and its people. Ask God to help you to see its people through his eyes.

Next Week

We ended this week with Jonah fleeing to Tarshish. Where was Tarshish? What kind of place was it? Not only will we learn about this port city but we will also learn everything you ever wanted to know about maritime trade in the ancient Near East.

Closing Prayer

Ask your group members if there is something they would like prayer for—especially something highlighted by this week's video. We recommend that your prayer secretary keep a running list so that the group can revisit past prayer requests and check in on how things are going. This is a great way for the group to get to know each other and bear each other's burdens.

Reminder: If you are behind in the reading, pick back up with Week Four, Day One tomorrow to get back on track.

SESSION 4

To Hurl or Not to Hurl

Debrief and Discover

As we saw last week, Jonah's plan is to escape from the presence of Yahweh. Think about that for a moment. Is it possible to hide from the presence of Yahweh?

View Session 4 Video: "To Hurl or Not to Hurl" (29 minutes)

The outline for this study is found on page 159 in the "Video Notes Guide" section. Have your group members turn there while watching the video. Encourage them to take notes and jot down questions and "aha" moments.

Launch Questions

- As you were asked in your study guide this week, what belief system rises to the top when you crash into a life crisis (like a calling that terrifies you)?
- Do you actually *believe* your God is omnipresent and omnipotent, or do you *really* believe something else (like you can hide from him in the hold of a ship)?

Dialogue and Digest

- In the lecture we learned that for the people of the ancient Near East the word "sea" is the name of a god and thus the sea is a person. And this god can be offended. So when the sailors learned that Jonah worshipped the God of land *and* sea they were terrified.
- Is the idea that the sea was a god in the ancient Near East new to you?

- How does this new knowledge affect your understanding of Jonah's response to the sailors when he tells them the only way to calm the storm is to hurl him into the sea? What, in effect, are they doing?

Decide and Do

- In the opening we asked if it is possible to hide from the presence of Yahweh, the God of land and sea, the Creator of the cosmos. Could Jonah hide from the presence of Yahweh? Read the words of the psalmist in Psalm 139:7–18.

Next Week

Our literary theme for this week was "to hurl." Next week, in our next chapter our new literary theme is "to appoint," and with this new literary theme we will get to explore the world of large aquatic mammals.

Closing Prayer

Ask your group members if there is something they would like prayer for—especially something highlighted by this week's video. Are you keeping a list yet?

Reminder: If you are behind in the reading, pick back up with Week Five, Day One tomorrow to get back on track.

SESSION 5

To Appoint

Debrief and Discover

Ask your members if any of them have had any experience with a large aquatic mammal (not including Sea World!). Do you think it is possible for one of these creatures to swallow a man whole *and* regurgitate said man whole and alive? I think of *Finding Nemo* when Dory and Marlin are in the mouth of the whale. Marlin obviously does *not* think it is possible. Dory, on the other hand, admits she doesn't know, but is willing to find out!

View Session 5 Video: "To Appoint" (28 minutes)

The outline for this study is found on page 161 in the "Video Notes Guide" section. Have your group members turn there while watching the video. Encourage them to take notes and jot down questions and "aha" moments.

Launch Questions

■ Okay, all you marine biologist types out there, how does this potential that a large, probably male, sperm whale might have been wandering around the Mediterranean at just the right moment to play the role of the most unlikely lifeguard of all time strike you? We know it's *possible* for a sperm whale to swallow an adult human, and to regurgitate him. How does the potential of him surviving the process impact you?

Dialogue and Digest

■ What struck you the most about the discussion of sperm whales?
■ Richter ends her discussion regarding the possibility of a human surviving being swallowed by a whale with this statement: "The

challenge, of course, would be for the man to survive. I think that would take a miracle. But you know what? I think that is exactly what this book is about." What miracles have you already observed in the book thus far?

Decide and Do

■ Turn back to Day Three in this week's study guide and re-read Eden Parker's lovely poem and listen to the possible thoughts of the whale.

Next Week

Next week we will get to see Jonah's response to being swallowed by a whale! What does he do inside the belly of great fish for three days and three nights? We will also see our next literary theme in the book of Jonah . . . "to announce."

Closing Prayer

Ask your group members if there is something they would like prayer for—especially something highlighted by this week's video. How's that list coming?

Reminder: If you are behind in the reading, pick back up with Week Six, Day One tomorrow to get back on track.

SESSION 6

A Second Chance

Debrief and Discover

On Day One of this week's study guide, your group members were asked if they have a Scripture passage or a song that gets them through difficult times. Ask your group if anyone would be willing to share that verse or song with the group.

View Session 6 Video: "A Second Chance" (28 minutes)

The outline for this study is found on page 163 in the "Video Notes Guide" section. Have your group members turn there while watching the video. Encourage them to take notes and jot down questions and "aha" moments.

Launch Questions

- Have you ever been in a place where you *really* wanted a do-over? You'd blown it, you knew it, and all you really wanted or needed was a second chance. Did you get one?

Dialogue and Digest

- Richter says: "I don't think this book has much at all to do with Nineveh. I think this book has a great deal to do with what a seasoned believer is learning about the character of his God." Do you agree or disagree with this statement? What have you observed so far in our study that supports your opinion?
- In Jonah's song of deliverance and psalm of praise we see that Jonah recognizes that he should have died and that God is giving him a second chance, a do-over. So when God calls a second time, Jonah

goes. If you responded yes to our launch question about getting a second chance, what did you do with your do-over?

Decide and Do

▨ Be encouraged. Our God *is* a God of second (and third and fourth and fifth) chances. For those times when you feel like you've blown it, remember: "The steadfast love of the LORD never ceases, his mercies never come to an end; they are new every morning; great is your faithfulness" (Lam. 3:22–23 NRSV).

Next Week

The moment we've all been waiting for . . . Jonah has gone to Nineveh and announced the message of Yahweh to its people! What will happen next?

Closing Prayer

Ask your group members if there is something they would like prayer for— especially something highlighted by this week's video.

Reminder: If you are behind in the reading, pick back up with Week Seven, Day One tomorrow to get back on track.

A Compassionate God and
a (Very) Angry Prophet

Debrief and Discover

Share the dictionary definition of "compassion" with your group: "sympathetic pity and concern for the sufferings or misfortunes of others." Ask your group members what comes to mind when they hear the word *compassion*.

View Session 7 Video: "A Compassionate God and a (Very) Angry Prophet" (28 minutes)

The outline for this study is found on page 165 in the "Video Notes Guide" section. Have your group members turn there while watching the video. Encourage them to take notes and jot down questions and "aha" moments.

Launch Questions

Leaders, once again, it is important that the following questions be asked, as they address the whole point of the book of Jonah. Answering the questions honestly can be a transformational learning moment for your group— especially now that they've already asked and answered the question once. Remember that the human condition is such that we all find some "other" group of people intimidating or even distasteful. For the young Latino girl, it might be the high school "jocks" walking toward her on that empty street. For a young white girl it might be the same. For the young Christian Arab girl in Afghanistan it might be a member of the "Committee for the Propagation of Virtue and the Prevention of Vice" (e.g., religious police). Be sensitive to your group. Be open to their legitimate fears and God's calling. Answer honestly . . . and think of Jonah.

- Name a group/type of people that you are afraid of. Why?
- What do you feel when you see someone from that group walking toward you on an empty street? Standing in line behind you at a convenience store or at an airport? Knocking on your front door?
- Do you think the God of Jonah has compassion on the person you have reason to fear and perhaps reason to hate?

Dialogue and Digest

- Richter says: "Here we have a crowd of people who are standing here in Nineveh and we had a crowd of people standing there on the ship who do not yet know what to expect from the God of Israel. And yet they have a prophet standing in their midst and he is not bothering to tell them who Yahweh is." In what ways does this statement challenge you? How often do you find yourself standing in a crowd of people who do not yet know what to expect from our God? Do you tell them? If not, what keeps you from doing so?

Decide and Do

- In Session 3 we asked you to pray for the people of the one city you would avoid at all costs. If you've been praying for them would you be willing to share how God has changed your heart/attitude toward these people?
- In today's launch question you were asked to name a group or type of people that you fear and perhaps even hate. Take some time to pray for them as well throughout this week.

Next Week

We've come to the climax of the book. Jonah has preached, the people have repented, Yahweh has had compassion . . . and Jonah is very angry. Next week we'll find out God's response to Jonah's anger.

Closing Prayer

Ask your group members if there is something they would like prayer for—especially something highlighted by this week's video.

Reminder: If you are behind in the reading, pick back up with Week Eight, Day One tomorrow to get back on track.

SESSION 8

Does Jonah Get It?

Debrief and Discover

In this week's study we read the following statement: If you were to ask a random person on the street the number-one reason they no longer go to church, the answer would be "Christians." Ask your group members if they agree or disagree with this statement and why.

View Session 8 Video: "Does Jonah Get It?" (27 minutes)

The outline for this study is found on page 167 in the "Video Notes Guide" section. Have your group members turn there while watching the video. Encourage them to take notes and jot down questions and "aha" moments.

Launch Questions

- Without placing blame at any one person or program's door, start the hard conversation about areas in your current church community where you are looking more like Jonah than Yahweh in the pursuit of the care and conversion of the Ninevites in your world.

Dialogue and Digest

- Richter challenges us: "I'm going to argue that the reason we've been given this book and the reason that this particular story about the official appointed public figure known as Jonah has wound up in our Bibles is that we're supposed to follow along with this line of questioning and we're supposed to be challenged right along with him. In comparison to 120,000 people and ten times that number in livestock, how in the world could Jonah, a believer, be that self-centered? . . . How can it be that we the people of God who are living

148

with the privileges of God can be so absorbed with our own needs that we can't see the faces of the people around us?"

■ Richter asks us: "Are the gifts and the graces that have been offered to the people of God only for the people of God, or are they for the folks of Nineveh as well?"

Decide and Do

■ "Save the Assyrians, save yourself." What does this mean? What are some practical ways we can do this? How can your group go about doing this?

Closing Prayer

Ask your group members if there is something they would like prayer for—especially something highlighted by this week's video.

Video Notes Guide

We have included an outline for each week's video lecture. These guides are designed to help organize the content of the video lectures for the group members. Our hope is that you will keep the outline in front of you as you view each of the lectures as a tool for following along, as well as a place to jot down notes and questions.

Introduction

I. Introductions!
    A. Your teacher: Sandra Richter, Robert H. Gundry Chair of Biblical Studies at Westmont College in Santa Barbara, CA
    B. Your objective: Get Jonah and his people back into real time and space so that we can hear God's message in the mix!

II. Perceptions of the Book?
    A. In the church
        1. Children's story
            a. A stodgy old prophet and a really big whale = a great story
            b. A moralism or two + some coloring pages = a children's church lesson
        2. Camp song
            a. "Who did, who did, who did, who did . . ."
            b. Fun fiction
    B. In the academy
        1. Allegory
            a. Jonah = Israel
            b. Whale = Babylon
            c. The vomiting = release from the exile
            d. Conversion of the Ninevites = the gospel going to the Gentiles
        2. Parable with a moral message
            a. Love your enemies!
            b. Nationalism is narrow!
            c. God's universal goals for evangelism!

3. Popular legend
   a. Eighth-century Israel could not have been advanced
      enough to challenge their own nationalism
   b. Hence, this book must be a fictional 4–5th century
      creation resulting from Israel getting past their national-
      istic bubble in the exile

III. What we're going to do
   A. Recognize that the God of Israel is very much in the practice of
      speaking a cross-cultural message to challenge his people
   B. Read the book as it was intended . . .
   C. In real space and time . . .
   D. As one of the Minor Prophets with a message of transformation
      for *us*!

SESSION 2

What Is a Prophet?

I. The office of the prophet in Israel
   A. The office
      1. Officer of the theocracy
      2. King-maker and king-breaker
   B. Terms applied in biblical studies?
      1. Former vs. latter
      2. Major vs. minor
         a. The book of Jonah is unique
            i. Not directed to Israel
            ii. Not a collection of sermons/oracles
            iii. Jonah's *life* is his message
            iv. "Did not get the point"
         b. The book of Jonah placed in the Prophets all the same
      3. Office vs. gift
         a. Gift: temporary anointing
         b. Office: the theocratic office
            i. Legislation of the theocracy
               a) Deuteronomy 13:1–5; the law of the suzerain
               b) Deuteronomy 18:9–15; of omens, lungs, and livers
               c) Deuteronomy 18:15; Moses is the prototype
            ii. Messenger of the divine council
               a) Decision-making body of the cosmos
               b) Isaiah 6:1–9; 1 Kings 22:6–8, 13–23; Jeremiah 23:18, 22; Amos 3:7

II.   Launch question: How does this understanding of what a prophet was in ancient Israel affect your read of Jonah's book? How about your read of Jonah's life? If you could ask one question about Jonah in light of this information, what would it be?

Who was the prophet of Israel? The diplomat of the Most High, litigator of the covenant lawsuit, and the conscience of the king.

The Cast of Characters: Jonah, Gath-hepher, and Jeroboam II versus the Nation of Assyria and the City of Nineveh

I. Who is Jonah?
    A. A historical note in 2 Kings 14:23–25
    B. Real space: Gath-hepher of Zebulun
    C. Real time: the prosperous days of Jeroboam II in the Northern Kingdom/Israel (8th century BCE)

II. What was Nineveh and who are the Assyrians?
    A. Nineveh
        1. Ancient royal city in Assyria
        2. Soon to be the *capital* of Assyria
    B. The Neo-Assyrian Empire
        1. The Rise of Tiglath-Pileser III, 745 BCE
        2. "Instituting a level of destruction that disallowed rebirth"
        3. The Black Obelisk of Shalmaneser III (858–824 BCE)
            a. Portrays King Jehu of the northern kingdom of Israel
            b. "Son of Omri"
            c. Brutality, exile, economic oppression
        4. The "Borg"/ISIS of the ancient Near East
        5. Nahum's "bloody city" (Nahum 3:1–3)

III. The word of the LORD came to Jonah son of Amittai: "Go to the great city of Nineveh and preach against it, because its wickedness has come up before me." But Jonah ran . . . (1:1–3)
   A. Does Jonah have a right to be afraid of these people?
   B. Does Jonah have a right to hate these people?

IV. Launch question: Name a group/type of people that you are afraid of. Be honest. What do you feel when you see someone from that group walking toward you on an empty street? Standing in line behind you at a convenience store or at an airport? Knocking on your front door?

"But instead, Jonah ran away from Yahweh and fled for Tarshish." (Jonah 1:3a, author's paraphrase)

SESSION 4

To Hurl or Not to Hurl

I. From Gath-hepher to Tarshish
   A. Most likely Tartessus in the south of Spain
      1. A trade emporium specializing in tin
      2. Approximately 2,000 miles west of Israel!
   B. Whereas Nineveh was 660 land miles *east* of Israel

II. Everything you ever wanted to know about maritime trade in the
    ancient Near East
   A. A standard Late Bronze Age (1500–1200 BCE) Phoenician
      trade ship
      1. The "Byblos Ship"
         a. A relief from Queen Hatshepsut's mortuary temple at
            Deir el Bahri (1479–1457 BC)
         b. Standard trade ship about 49 feet long
         c. Standard war ship about 75 feet long (and narrow)
   B. Did the ancients sail the open seas?
   C. What were the trade items?
      1. Our folks were exporting timber, oil, and wine
      2. Desert caravans added ivory, spices, apes, and wild animal
         skins
      3. Queen Hatshepsut's temple relief shows the "marvels from
         the land of Punt"—fragrant woods, myrrh-resin, ebony, ivory,
         green gold, cosmetics, "natives and their children"
   D. Underwater archaeology has given us Late Bronze shipwrecks
      1. Bronze swords, arrowheads, and stone maces
      2. Ostrich eggshells, ivory, pottery, fishing nets
      3. Ingots of raw metal, exotic wood, aromatic resin

III. Our first chapter and our first literary theme: to "hurl" (*tûl* טול)

    A. Our God *hurls* the wind at the ship (v. 4)

    B. Creating a storm that *terrified* professional sailors

        1. Each sailor cries out to his god (v. 5)

        2. The sailors *hurl* the cargo (their livelihood!) into the sea (v. 5)

        3. The sailors cast lots and the lot falls on Jonah (v. 7)

    C. The nature of "sea" in the mind of an ancient polytheist

        1. A living deity not just a "thing"

        2. The portal to Hades

        3. Jonah identifies himself as a "Hebrew" (v. 9)

        4. Jonah identifies Yahweh as the God of land and sea (v. 9)

IV. Launch question: As you were asked in your study guide this week, what belief system rises to the top when you crash into a life crisis (like a calling that terrifies you)? Do you actually *believe* your God is omnipresent and omnipotent, or do you *really* believe something else (like you can hide from him in the hold of a ship)?

"So Yahweh hurled a great wind toward the sea so that there was a great storm on the sea, and the ship was about to break up." (Jonah 1:4, author's paraphrase)

SESSION 5

To Appoint

I. Chapter 1 continued: the literary theme is to "hurl" (*tûl* טול)
   A. The sailors *hurled* Jonah overboard (v. 15)
      1. Hurling was not their first choice
      2. The sailors cried out to Yahweh for forgiveness
      3. Finally hurl Jonah overboard and see immediate results
   B. "At this the men greatly *feared* [Yahweh], and they offered a sacrifice to [Yahweh] and made vows to him." (v. 16, emphasis added)
      1. Jonah's first missionary act has been accomplished; these men are, at some level, converted
      2. Yahweh has secured his witness from his unwilling missionary

II. Chapter 2: the literary theme is to "appoint" (*mānāh* מנה)
   A. God *appoints* a "great fish" (1:17 English / 2:1 Hebrew)
   B. How does a "great fish" become a whale?
   C. Everything you ever wanted to know about "great fish" swallowing humans
      1. A PhD candidate, a L'Abri center, and an assigned topic
         a. A. A. Berzin on *The Sperm Whale*
         b. A whole bunch of "big fish" people on the East Coast
      2. Regarding sharks: the Great White
         a. Frequent the Mediterranean and reach 25 feet long
         b. Feeding habit is such that very little comes out of that mouth alive

3. Regarding whales: the sperm whale
    a. Frequent the Mediterranean and can reach 63 feet long
    b. Feeding habit is to gulp up a bunch of stuff, squeeze out the excess water in their first stomach, and eventually throw up the oddities they didn't mean to catch
    c. Favorite meal? The giant squid!
4. Some testimonials from the whaling industry of the 1800–1900s
    a. James Bartley from *Star of the East* in 1891
    b. Egerton Y. Davis Jr. report from the *Toulinguet* off of St. John's, Newfoundland
    c. Marshall Jenkins 1771 from an Edgartown USA whaling vessel

III. Launch question: Okay, all you marine biologist types out there, how does this potential that a large, probably male, sperm whale might have been wandering around the Mediterranean at just the right moment to play the role of the most unlikely lifeguard of all time strike you? We know it's *possible* for a sperm whale to swallow an adult human, and to regurgitate him. How does the potential of him surviving the process impact you?

Jonah will die. And this missionary who feared martyrdom now faces execution at the hand of his own God.

" In the Whale " - Documentary

SESSION 6

A Second Chance

I. Chapter 2 continued: to "appoint" (*mānāh* מנה)
   A. Yahweh *appointed* a prophet to go and preach to Nineveh, but he *rebelled*
   B. Next Yahweh *appointed* a great fish to go and retrieve his prophet, the fish *obeyed*
      1. Jonah's song of deliverance (2:2–6)
         a. The belly of Sheol
         b. Water encompassed me
         c. The primeval deep engulfed me
         d. God hears and delivers
      2. Jonah's song compared to Psalm 18
         a. Cords of death encompassed me
         b. The torrents of ungodliness terrified me
         c. The cords of Sheol wrapped around me
         d. He heard my cry . . . he delivered me
      3. Jonah's psalm of praise (2:7–9)
         a. Remembered the Lord
         b. Sacrifice and vows
   C. Then Yahweh spoke to the fish (2:10)
      1. Jonah tossed out on the dry land exactly where Yahweh wanted him to go in the first place!
      2. Jonah is given a second chance

II. Our next chapter and our next literary theme: to "announce" (*qārā'* קרא)
   A. Yahweh speaks to Jonah a second time: "Go to Nineveh . . . and *announce* to it" (3:1–2)
   B. This time, Jonah goes

    C. Nineveh, "the great city" (3:2–3, author's paraphrase)
        1. Not yet the capital, but a longstanding royal city
        2. 1,850 acres, 15 gates—each named for a deity
           a. The second largest city in the ancient Near East
           b. But "three days" in the text is hotly debated
           c. The city is not large enough to take three days to traverse, but D. J. Wiseman notes that this is the standard length of visit for a diplomat
           d. Another reading is to read a textual error that would have communicated that it took Jonah "thirty days" to travel there
        3. For Jonah this vast and elegant city would have been overwhelming!

III.   Launch Question: Have you ever been in a place where you *really* wanted a do-over? You'd blown it, you knew it, and all you really wanted or needed was a second chance. Did you get one?

And so Jonah, the great man of God who has intentionally, willfully defied the command of his God, is given a second chance.

A Compassionate God and a (Very) Angry Prophet

I. Chapter 3 continues with the theme word: to "announce"
    (*qārā'* קרא)

    A. Jonah's "cognitive dissonance"

        1. He believes the gifts of God are designed for the people of God

        2. Yet he is learning that God's plan reaches to the edge of the globe

    B. Jonah's preaching

        1. Jonah *announces*: "Forty more days and Nineveh will be over-thrown" (3:4)

        2. "The Ninevites believed God" (3:5)

            a. In real time, Assyria is in a very vulnerable place (782–745 BCE)

                i.   Militarily: war with Urartu to the north

                ii. Economically: famines in 765 and 763 BC

                iii. Spiritually: eclipse of the sun June 15, 763 BC

            b. Mourning with sackcloth and ashes in the ancient world (see study guide!)

            c. "Who knows? God may yet relent [from his wrath] and with compassion turn from his fierce anger so that we will not perish" (3:9)

                i.   Compare this statement with the sailors

                ii. What is our narrator doing?

            d. The Ninevites repent

                i.   Isn't this the goal?

                ii. Why isn't Jonah pleased?

II. Chapter 4: a compassionate God and a (very) angry prophet
   A. Jonah was "very displeased, with a great displeasure, and he became angry" (4:1, author's paraphrase)
   B. Why is Jonah angry?

III. Launch question: Name a group/type of people that you are afraid of. Why? What do you feel when you see someone from that group walking toward you on an empty street? Standing in line behind you at a convenience store or at an airport? Knocking on your front door? Do you think the God of Jonah has compassion on the person you have reason to fear and perhaps reason to hate?

"because I knew that you are a God of grace and compassion, slow to anger and abundant in lovingkindness, and one who repents of evil" (Jonah 4:2b, author's paraphrase)

SESSION 8

Does Jonah Get It?

I. Jonah's displeasure; evil (*rā'āh* רָעָה in the book of Jonah)
   A. Evil is complex
   B. Evil in the book of Jonah
      1. Jonah 1:2—their *wickedness* has come up before me
      2. Jonah 1:7–8—this *calamity* that has struck us
      3. Jonah 3:7—the *evil* that is in their hands
      4. Jonah 3:10—then God relented concerning the *calamity* which he had declared
      5. Jonah's evil in 4:1—and it was *evil* to Jonah, very *evil*, and he became angry (author's own; see your study guide!)

II. God appoints (*mānāh* מנה)
   A. A plant to be a shade to deliver Jonah from his *discomfort* (*rā'āh*) (4:6)
   B. A worm to attack the plant (4:7)
   C. A scorching east wind and "the sun blazed on Jonah's head" (4:8)
   D. And Jonah begged with all his soul to die, saying, "Death is better to me than life" (4:8, author's paraphrase)

III. God speaks to Jonah (4:9–11)

IV. How . . .
   A. Could Jonah be more concerned about himself than the Ninevites?
   B. Could we be more concerned about ourselves than those around us?

V.   What if . . .
    A. There were a fifth chapter of Jonah?
    B. Jonah had gone home and brought back a team of Levites to disciple the Assyrians?
    C. "Save the Assyrians, save yourselves"

VI.   The message of Jonah's book
    A. Yahweh is truly the Lord of the cosmos
    B. God's servants are in his hands
    C. Yahweh cares about every man, woman, and child on this planet, even the enemies of the kingdom of God

VII.   Launch question: Without placing blame at any one person or program's door, start the hard conversation about areas in your current church community where you are looking more like Jonah than Yahweh in the pursuit of the care and conversion of the Ninevites in your world.

In sum, to contradict Archibald Asparagus, there has been no mistake, no misunderstanding. The word of God is not just for the people of God. It is for the lost. It is even for the enemies of the kingdom. In the book of Jonah, Jonah is delivered from the consequences of his own sin. He ran, and he nearly died as a result. Yet when Jonah cried out to God, God saved him. The message of Jonah's book is that God will do no less for the citizens of Nineveh.

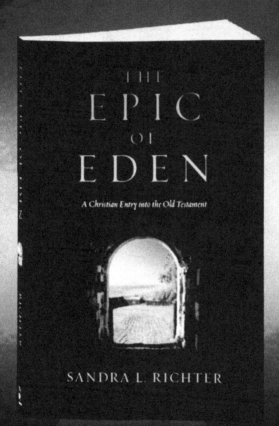

Printed in the USA
CPSIA information can be obtained
at www.ICGtesting.com
LVHW041040170923
758037LV00002B/4